Drawn In:

Dramatic Encounters With Art

Michael G. Bausch

About the cover photo:

An artist painting her copy of a canvas hanging in a gallery of the Musée du Louvre, Paris. Photo by Michael Bausch.

Please contact Michael Bausch for written permission to photocopy or reproduce any of this material through www.michaelgbausch.com.

DEDICATION

To my wife, Catherine Ann Carlson, who first drew me into some of the world's finest art museums and who encouraged my many years of travel and study.

CONTENTS

ACKNOWLEDGMENTS 1

DRAWN IN 2

BEAUTIFUL THINGS 8

FLORENCE: *DAVID* 16

VENICE: INNOCENTS 24

ROME: ST. PETER'S CHAIR 34

ROME: CARAVAGGIO 41

SAINT OBELISK 53

SICILY: SHORT POEMS 84

BERKELEY: ABU GHRAIB 90

AVATAR (2009) 93

END NOTES 104

ACKNOWLEDGMENTS

As with any book project, there are special people to thank:

— Wilson Yates, who kindly encouraged my developing journey into painting, sculpture, and architecture as my advisor in the Doctor of Ministry program of the United Theological Seminary of the Twin Cities. He approved my independent reading and travel adventures to Italy.

— The late professor Doug Adams, who enthusiastically endorsed my early writing about art and film, advocated for my teaching summer sessions and online courses through the Pacific School of Religion in Berkeley, California, and welcomed me with generous hospitality when I visited his classes.

— E. Martin Pedersen, who as friend, writer, and professor living in Sicily, guided and drove me for a month of travels throughout Italy.

— The late Tom and Margo Zerbel, who trusted me to be their guide in Rome, Florence, and Venice as members of my first tour group, and all the others who followed them!

— Fred Noer of Image Source, for his keen eye, copy-editing, and editorial advice with this project.

1

Chapter 1

DRAWN IN

Until about the age of forty, when anyone said anything to me about "the arts" I immediately thought about music, television, or film. I had very little experience with the visual arts of paintings, sculptures, or architecture, and I seldom, if ever, visited art museums.

That all changed when my wife Cathy suggested we take a trip to Europe, which would include going to the museums she had grown to love. We went to Amsterdam in 1990, and on my first morning there she drew me into the Rijksmuseum. Even though I was suffering from jet lag, more than her, she patiently shared her excitement about what we were seeing and helped me see things in paintings I had never noticed.

The next day we went back. The day after that we went to the Van Gogh Museum. Two years later she got me to the Louvre, the Picasso, the Orangeries, the Rodin, and the d'Orsay in Paris. While she didn't know it at the time, she was teaching me to see paintings and sculpture in fresh, new ways.

Within a year of those experiences I took a month to visit Italy with a friend who was living there, and he and I traveled through Sicily for two weeks and then went on to the rest of Italy. All along the way we stopped in every museum we found, including smaller ones in Sicily, and the big ones in the large cities: the Vatican Museum in Rome, the Uffizi, and the Accademia in Florence and Venice.

Along the way we stopped in churches and saw more

paintings and sculptures as well as magnificent and even monumental architecture.

After my month was up, I couldn't wait to return, and I began thinking of ways to bring others with me in small group tours. I found one couple who'd go with me the following year, and then over the years the groups grew in size. I began to organize other trips that took me and these travelers to other cities and their museums: London, Madrid, Barcelona, Bilbao, Toledo, Strasbourg, Colmar, Cairo, Jerusalem, Athens, Samos.

Within a year after that first month's immersion, I was enrolling in a doctoral program at the United Theological Seminary of the Twin Cities, and over the course of three years I took courses where I read about art, wrote about my experiences with art, attended conferences about art, and brought together children, youth, and adults to experience, discuss, and create art.

Just as I was drawn into art by the "pushes" and "pulls" of others who encouraged me along the way, I too began to push and pull others into this fascinating world.

The original title for this little book was to be something like "Italian Immersions: Encounters With Art." In a flash of whimsy, though, and thinking about my story of how I became engaged with art, I thought of the title, "Drawn In."

It's true that good art draws us in – to linger, to question, to discuss, to simply enjoy. It's also true the artist has "drawn" into an artwork a lifetime of study, practice, reading, and a world of stories and themes. I hope you are drawn into this book as much as I've been drawn into what I'm about to share!

Beautiful Things in Florence, Venice, and Rome (Chapters 1, 2, 3, 4, 5)

After starting a Doctor of Ministry program at the Minnesota Consortium of Theological Schools in Minneapolis/St. Paul, I'd also organized a trip to Rome, Florence, and Venice with two travelers.

Why not be efficient and use the time in Italy to begin an independent study in art appreciation? I set some learning goals centered around three works of art: a sculpture, a painting, and an altar piece.

I started reading art history and books on how to interpret the meanings in works of art. As I read in preparation for my second visit to Italy, one theme that kept surfacing was the difference between "looking at" art and "seeing" art, or the difference between a quick look at a work of art and an attentive study (see Chapter 1, "Beautiful Things").

Then I applied what I learned to the study of three works of art, one in Rome, one in Florence, and one in Venice (see Chapters 3, 4, 5 and 6).

The fruits of my labor were then reported to my professor in July 1994, and for the next 20 years I used what I'd learned as part of my guiding more than 20 small groups to Italy.

St. Obelisk (Chapter 6)

A second project grew out of the first one. When I found a connection with the obelisk in the center of St. Peter's Square to the events surrounding the death of Peter, the Galilean fisherman who followed Jesus of Nazareth and who wound up dying a martyr in the capital of the Roman Empire, I became even more curious.

I wanted to learn all I could about the needle-shaped piece of stone so prominently located in front of St. Peter's Basilica. Where did the obelisk come from? What did it mean to the ancient Egyptians who first used it in their own religious architecture? What did it mean to the Romans who brought it from Egypt to this place, and what did it symbolize to the Pope, who had the thing moved from its original location? Finally, what might it mean today?

For this study I did research via a small local public library, gaining access to books on the subject of obelisks through interlibrary loan, mostly from university collections. This was before the internet, although I was able to use a primitive dial-up connection with a laptop computer to access university library catalogs through a portal offered with an 800 number by the University of Minnesota. I could get book titles that way and then go to my local public library and order them.

A whole world of Egyptian, Roman, and papal history emerged. I began discovering the story behind the granite needle standing in the middle of St Peter's Square in Rome, including how the needle was originally brought to serve as a centerpiece on the spine of an emperor's chariot track.

This report, like the previous one, was developed in partial completion of requirements for the doctor of ministry degree.

Calling of St. Matthew (Chapter 7)

This project grew out of an experience I had with this Caravaggio painting in the Contarelli Chapel in the church of San Luigi dei Francesi in Rome. After an unexpected lesson in perspective, I bought a postcard of the painting in the church and brought the postcard home with me, where I studied the painting for a good week.

As I looked at the tiny copy of the picture, it began to dawn on me that Caravaggio had, with brush and oil paint, "written" into the picture a group of at least ten verses from the Gospel of Matthew. He was telling a story without writing it down!

I wrote the results of my study in a paper that also counted toward partial completion of requirements for the doctor of ministry degree. Since then, I have shared what I learned with students taking university-level courses in New Testament studies, in seminars with other pastors, and in sermons.

Verses From Sicily (Chapter 8)

These short poems are the results of my paying attention to what's going on around me while traveling in Sicily my first time, with all senses keenly heightened. I hope the poems offer you a little breather after the density of some of what came before in the earlier chapters!

Berkeley: *Abu Ghraib* (Chapter 9)

My immersions with art, sculpture, and architecture in Italy helped prepare me for other experiences with art. While spending a semester in Berkeley as a "minister in residence" at the Pacific School of Religion, I enjoyed full access to the resources of the University of California and of the Graduate Theological Union.

Shortly after my arrival on campus, I learned that the Colombian artist Fernando Botero was to speak about his recent paintings responding to the punishments inflicted by U.S. soldiers on Iraqis held captive at the Abu Ghraib prison, located just west of Baghdad.

I went to hear Botero speak and then toured his exhibit housed at the Bancroft Library of the University of California Library, and this short article is my report on what Botero had to say.

Avatar (2009) (Chapter 10)

Developing *saper vedere* ("learning how to see") skills carries over into other arts as well, including film. I've practiced a simple way to understand any work of art, including film, by identifying the form, content, and meaning of the art. The form is the thing itself, what it is. The content is the story and the details that are included in its telling. The meaning is the lesson or the moral to the story, the "so what" of the work of art or the film.

When I go to a movie I take a pen and notebook and write (in the dark!) anything that catches my attention. I watch for things like short "sermons" in the dialogue as well as references to scripture, other art, literature, and music. Later, I try to figure out what they mean.

In James Cameron's worldwide box office hit *Avatar*, I found biblical references and parallels as well an apparent revival of an ancient theological debate.

Chapter 2

BEAUTIFUL THINGS

Shortly after drilling a hole into the newly discovered tomb wall in Egypt's Valley of the Kings, archaeologist Howard Carter inserted a candle and peered into an ancient room. When asked if he could see anything, he breathed, "Yes, wonderful things." It would be ten years before he understood all the implications of what he saw when he first looked into the treasure-filled royal tomb of the boy king Tutankhamun. (1)

When I first visited the Basilica of St. Peter in Rome, sampled the works of the versatile Michelangelo from Florence, or studied a haunting canvas by Bonifacio in Venice, it was like looking through a small hole by candlelight and reporting that I had seen wonderful things. One year later, after reading about art, its history, and interpretation, I could return to those Italian places and begin to uncover treasures beyond what I could have imagined.

I would have to return to St. Peter's on a Sunday morning to notice that Bernini's stained glass dove, representing the creative and revelatory power of the divine, directs its gaze in a laser-like beam through the baldacchino that shelters the high altar placed over the tomb of Peter, out the center door of the basilica, and directly to the ancient cross-topped obelisk that stands in the elliptical "square" outside.

The obelisk, all that remains above ground of Nero's circus, was quarried and carved in Egypt when the Hebrews were slaves and later brought to Rome during the time of Jesus. Thirty years later it stood mutely as Christians were crucified for their crimes or burned as torches to light the night for the Roman audience.

Topped now by a tiny cross, this symbol of imperial domain is neutralized, its power reduced to a decoration subservient to the dove-like Spirit of life whose black eyes beam from the circle of golden glass centered in the apse of Christendom's most famous church.

Or, I would have to stand in line thirty minutes outside the Accademia before being admitted to see the splendor of Florence-Michelangelo's version of Apollo/Hercules named *David* (2), after the slayer of the giant, the protector of Israel.

To really "see" that statue one first must walk through a gauntlet of carved "prisoners" as they try to break free from the marble that encases them, or stand mute before the strength of the Belvedere Torso in the Vatican Museum, or to have recognized the difference between the Apollo Belvedere and the Laocoon in the same museum, or compared Michelangelo's Florentine David with Bernini's Borghese *David* in Rome.

And in Venice, to return to the Accademia to find again the intriguing *The Slaughter of the Innocents* painted by Bonifacio De' Pitati (Bonifacio Veronese), and that this work and one other nearby seem to follow the compositional style of the better-known Giorgione, which alerts the viewer to the personal and historical changes that lie ahead.

Like Howard Carter, who needed to prepare well for what he might see next, I as art student needed to prepare myself for a way of seeing that would unlock some of the secrets of the treasures I would view.

This "way of seeing" is different from simply "looking." Jane Dillenberger suggests that "looking at" is a process of identification and recognition. Seeing, different from looking, involves "the whole range of experience and the wellsprings of one's being." (3)

An example of simply looking is found in the recent phenomenon of *The Magic Eye.* On the *New York Times* bestseller list for 40 weeks, this is a book of computer-generated colored designs. The viewer is instructed to "use your MAGIC EYE in a quiet, meditative time and place." (4)

To see the three-dimensional pictures within the colored design the viewer needs to concentrate, relax, and clear the mind. When this is accomplished, marvelous things appear, and for me it is an experience of joy and discovery. Yet because the design gives way to a hidden yet predetermined picture, it requires "a complex process in which visual cues are matched to an immense storehouse of optical memories, allowing an almost instantaneous recognition to take place." (5) This is looking, not seeing.

In the book *The Ultimate Alphabet,* artist Mike Wilks observes: "Looking is not the same as seeing. We are all proficient at looking but very poor at seeing. People who study such things calculate that the average person in an art gallery will spend six seconds in front of each picture...If we merely look at a painting then I am surprised that it will hold our attention for this long, but if we see it then we might be lost within it forever." (6)

Theologian Paul Tillich frequently referred to this kind of "seeing" experience as analogous to a revelation during his encounter with Botticelli's Madonna and Child with Angels: "As I stood there, bathed in the beauty its painter had envisioned so long ago, something of the divine source of all things came through to me." (7) Simply looking at that picture would have given him a sense of awe and beauty, but seeing it in contrast to his recent experience in the trenches of World War I brought him an ecstatic sense of order and hope.

Developing a "seeing" relationship with a work of art is similar to how we develop relationships with people. In her book, *Anatomy of Love*, Helen Fisher observes how a relationship with a person develops through a progression of activities that start with gazing, or looking, and then move to really "seeing." In her observations of behavior of men and women at singles bars Fisher says people move through five stages of courtship: 1) attention-getting 2) eye contact 3) talking 4) touch 5) body synchrony. (8)

The "courtship" with a work of art is similar:

1) A piece draws our attention by prior reputation or by something that catches our eye.

2) We begin to look at it more fully and if it is something intriguing to us, or something we wish to get to know, we will spend more time with it.

3) We will begin the process of communication, "talking" by beginning to ask questions internally about the artist's mood, the content, the form, the composition, technique, etc.

4) If we begin to find some answers, or see the painting in new ways, we begin to gain the excitement of discovery and communication.

5) The final stage is to be so enamored with the work of art that we are fully a part of it and almost mimic the work with our body.

I have seen this happen on two occasions, once at the Uffizi Gallery in Florence where a young woman stood in the same posture as Botticelli's Venus in *The Birth of Venus* as she viewed the painting, and once at the Louvre when I noticed two women standing in profile as they viewed a painting of three women in profile – a true body synchrony.

What happens during this final stage in the courtship with a work of visual art is what Jane Dillenberger calls "an exhilarating expansion of understanding. Momentarily, we see with the artist's eyes and feel with the artist's pulsebeat." (9)

This "aesthetic moment," as Bernard Berenson calls it, is that moment "when the spectator is at one with the work of art he is looking at . . . the two become one entity . . . ." (10)

How does one prepare for that moment? We might take a cue from Leonardo, whose curiosity and innovation were founded upon and shared by "what he called *saper vedere* (knowing how to see)." (11)

In his book, *Meaning In The Visual Arts*, Erwin Panofsky suggests that certain *saper vedere* skills need to be developed by the art historian to distinguish him or herself from the "naive beholder." (12)

The art historian:

– knows "his cultural equipment . . . would not be in harmony with that of people in another land and of a different period."

– makes "adjustments by learning as much as he possibly can of the circumstances under which the objects of his studies were created."

– will "collect and verify all the available factual information as to medium, condition, age, authorship, destination . . . (and) will also compare the work with others of its class and will examine such writings as they reflect the aesthetic standards of its country and age."

– will " . . . read old books on theology or mythology in order to identify its subject matter . . . determine its historical locus and to separate the individual contribution of its maker . . . ."

– will " . . . study the formal principles which control the rendering of the visible world."

– will " . . . observe the interplay between the influences of literary sources . . . in order to establish a history of iconographic formulae . . . ."

– will " . . . familiarize himself with the social, religious, and philosophical attitudes of other periods and countries, in order to correct his own subjective feeling for content."

– brings a familiarity with classical languages such as Latin, Greek, German, French, and Italian.

Such preparation, while intensive and exhaustive, will result in ways of seeing visual arts that ultimately bring the fullest interpretation and pleasure. It brings to birth that "aesthetic moment":

"The informed mind and attentive eye provide the 'Open, Sesame' for the vivifying moment when the barriers between our world and the artist's vision disappear. Momentarily, then, we see with the artist's eye and feel with his or her pulsebeat." (13)

In order to apply these lessons about the difference between "looking" and "seeing" I decided to focus my attention upon three pieces by artists who give their works a unique way of "seeing":

1. Michelangelo's *David* in Florence's Accademia and its "I can take this guy" kind of look in the eyes as he assesses Goliath and whatever other challenges lay ahead.

2. Bonifacio's *Slaughter of the Innocents* in the Accademia of Venice, in which several characters observe the massacre (described in the New Testament Gospel of Matthew, chapter 2) with a relaxed nonchalance and seem to be looking at, but not seeing, the chaos nearby.

3. Bernini's *Cathedra Petri* in the Basilica of St. Peter, particularly the stained-glass dove whose small, black eyes seem to pierce the basilica with confidence and strength.

My selections provided a happy challenge because they led me to learn what I could about each artist, each period, and each medium and to search out similar works of art for comparative observations. I tried to take seriously Professor Yates' four factors involved in the interpretative process:

" . . . information regarding the artist, the historical context of a work, the art school or style from which it comes, the elements of the work's composition and their relationship to the work's meaning . . . ." (14)

Each piece represents a different medium, a different artistic period, and a different setting: Michelangelo's *David*, a carved marble sculpture from the Florentine High Renaissance; Bonifacio's oil on canvas painting from the Venetian High Renaissance; Bernini's marble, bronze, stained glass, and gilt stucco apse in St. Peter's from the Baroque period he fathered in Rome.

The next three chapters offer my observations of the three pieces.

Chapter 3

FLORENCE: *DAVID*

DAVID, Michelangelo Buonarotti, 14 feet, carved marble, 1501-04, Accademia, Florence.

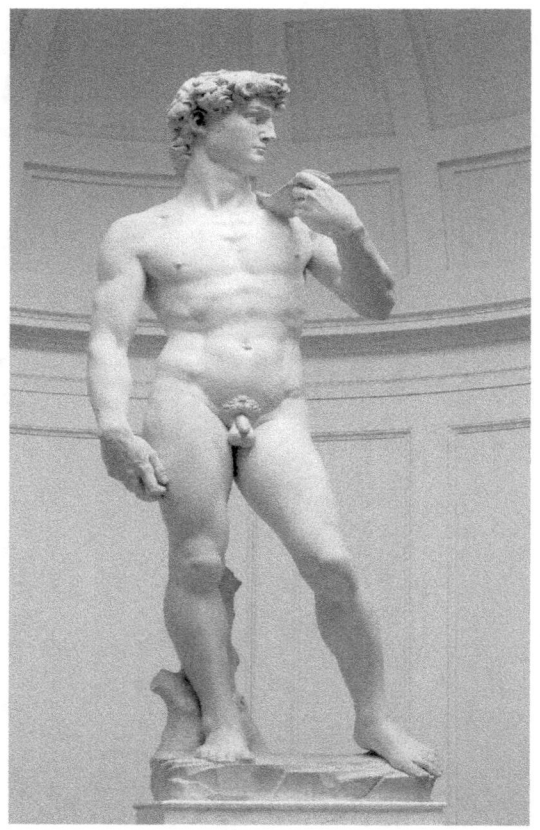

Photo credit: Rico Heil. Used under Creative Commons License GNU-FDL.

The first time I saw *David* was the copy that stands where the original was once placed, in Florence's Palazzo Vecchio. The occasion was an evening ceremony in June 1993 celebrating the re-opening of the Uffizi Museum following the May 1993 car bombing that had devastated one wing of the museum and killed a caretaker and his children. Relatives of the dead, city officials, various branches of the Italian police forces, ordinary citizens, and a few of us tourists all gathered in testimony to the resilient spirit of the people of Florence. Standing silently over the gathering was the copy of Michelangelo's *David*, fulfilling its centuries-old symbolic function for the city of Florence, "personifying the two main civic virtues of the Renaissance, Wrath and Strength." (15)

The copy of *David* stands in that square, reminding the people that they are guided and protected by a spirit of confidence and strength as well as an implicit willingness to fight for life, dignity, and honor.

Even the eyes of the copy convey the "I can take this guy" (16) confidence that the Florentines shared as they helped propel the rest of Italy into the Renaissance.

We stood in a line that was two city blocks long to get into the Accademia where the original is housed. Once inside, many people gathered around the statue, some trying to duplicate the beauty with their own photographs and videos. Those in the tour groups seemed to walk in a long line all the way around the statue, spending only seconds in study.

Others sat and contemplated. My visual study included viewing photographs of the statue some weeks prior to the trip and then studying the actual statue from different angles and distances in the Accademia.

David is young, lean, and muscular. Stripped naked, his only covering is the thin strap of the sling stretched tightly on his back. His left hand holds the sling, while the right measures the weight and smoothness of the stones. His right leg is tucked comfortably against a small tree trunk. All the attributes of the biblical David are communicated through the marble (see I Samuel 17 for the following details): the feeling of the invincibility of youth, a comfort with a self that is born of the solitude of the shepherd's days and nights, a confidence learned from hours of practice with the sling and from battle with lions and bears. (Funny, there are no scars visible on this, or any other, *David*!)

He transcends the negativity of his older brothers and Saul and is able to stand firm in the face of the belittling Goliath. He steps back to assess the situation, feeling the stones, taking the measure of his opponent, and instantaneously deciding to act.

From the eyes come a concentrated focus, a calm, and a strength, intensified by the knitting of the brow as an initial recognition of the imminent battle.

Centered by his experiences in the barren Judean wilderness, by solitude, by his love of music, poetry, and language, this *David* represents the renaissance man, schooled in classical languages, a lover, a poet, an artist, and an actor stepping forward into a different world.

It is a time of transition from the medieval view that God is in control to one founded upon a renewed Greco-Roman humanism that invites human beings to take their place next to (the gods) God as partners in creative effort.

I found it helpful to visually divide *David* in halves, first vertically, and then horizontally, to analyze the energy of the statue. Divided vertically, I notice that the left side of *David* is relaxed and quiet, while the right side is active and getting ready. The veins, tendons, and muscles are swelling in the right arm, as the body is powering up for action.

Divided horizontally, the lower body and legs stand gracefully, like those of a dancer, while the upper body shows concentrated energy. From the rear, one can see the bulge of the triceps in the left arm and can see the weight of the body centered on the right leg as it curves into the small stump for light support. While the right leg, rear view, appears relaxed, it is clear that here is where the weight of the body is carried.

The observer senses that the next action will be taken by the left leg, moving to the ball of the left foot as the stone is to be slung at Goliath. From the rear, the top half of the statue appears frozen, while the bottom half is activated with the anticipated simultaneous movement of the left leg and the right hand.

Michelangelo knew the human body. The ear canals are large and open, and all senses on alert. The nostrils are open and the abdomen deflated, so we know this *David* is not breathing in, but has just quietly exhaled, at the point of breath relaxation. There are strength in the thick, curly hair and understated intelligence in the classical elongation of the second toe of each foot. The fingernails are clean and clipped on the well-manicured hand of a gentleman, as seen most clearly on the thumb of the right hand.

From the right profile, the cheek is smooth and young looking, expressing calm even as the vein in the neck shows looming action. The veins along the right arm and hand combine action with grace, calm, and quiet.

From a distance, the upper body's chest musculature seems to show better, and the ribs and abdominal muscles become evident. Realizing that Michelangelo intended to place this *David* on a buttress of the Florence Duomo (17), we can see that the enlarged hand would focus the energy for the viewer far off — the very power of God is in that hand as the head confidently looks out at those distant Italian states that might threaten Florence's dominion. In the neo-platonic climate of the day, Michelangelo set up a kind of dialogue between the spirit or soul that was yearning to be set free from its body. In the *Pieta* nearby, we sense the weight of the dead Jesus and can see no air in the stomach, no life, and yet there is strength in his arm.

Even as the body is dead, the complete strength is not yet set free. In the unfinished face of the one who holds him, compared with the peace on the face of Jesus, we realize that the Jesus who is "finished" and whose work is done becomes the Christ whose strength endures. Matter and spirit remain in relationship in this sculpture.

The "prisoners" nearby struggle to become free from their marble prisons. The statues are more tentative and deliberately more roughly hewn than *David* and more clearly express the struggle of ideas/the soul as they seek to break free from material confinements. *David* seems to unify matter with spirit, hence the brilliance of the statue, as we see matter ready to spring into action, while simultaneously noticing spiritual purpose in the fiery concentration of the eyes of the statue.

An ancient model for this is the *Apollo Belvedere* in the Vatican Museum, a calm figure, in contrapposto, and frozen in pre-action, prior to sending an arrow into a wild animal beyond.

Michelangelo similarly expresses his figures in this calm, centered, and concentrated fashion. But he gives his Apollo fierce life, particularly in the eyes.

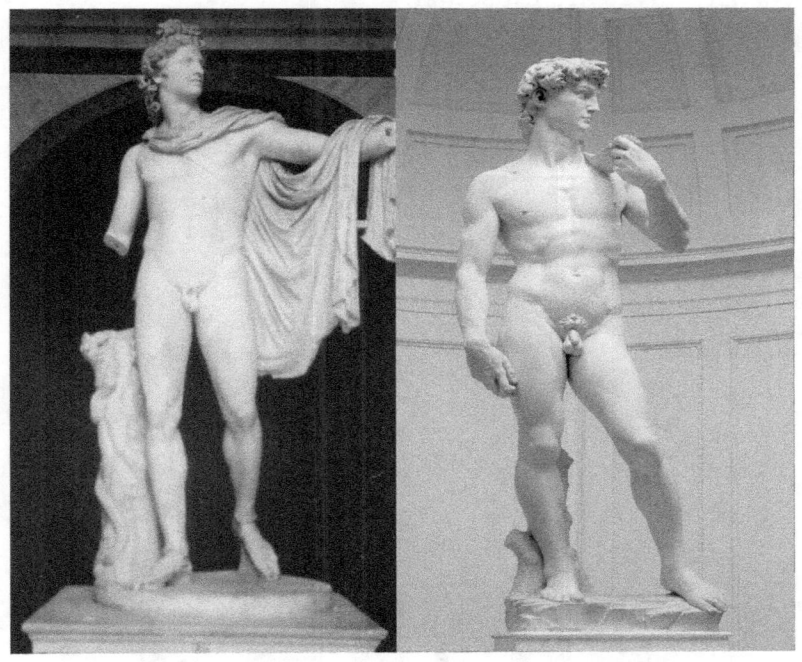

Photo credits: *Apollo* by Michael Bausch, *David* by Rico Heil.

Contrast this with Bernini's *David*, which is more like the *Laocoon* group (18) (discovered in Rome in 1506), swirling with action and in the heat of battle. Bernini, working in a different time, crafts figures exploding in action and passion. Long hair blows outward in the active moment (see his *Apollo and Daphne*), and tears flow (*Rape of Proserpina*).

For his *David*, in contrast to Michelangelo's, the figure is already in battle. Goliath is more present than ever, though still unseen.

Both eyes are blazing, the mouth is squeezed in determination, and the upper lip is puffed out with air. The vein is swollen in the left arm, the triceps expanded, and the brow is squeezed in effort. Veins pop in the right biceps and left wrist; calves are muscular.

He stands over his eagle-headed lyre upon which he has dropped the coat of mail and helmet Saul gave him.

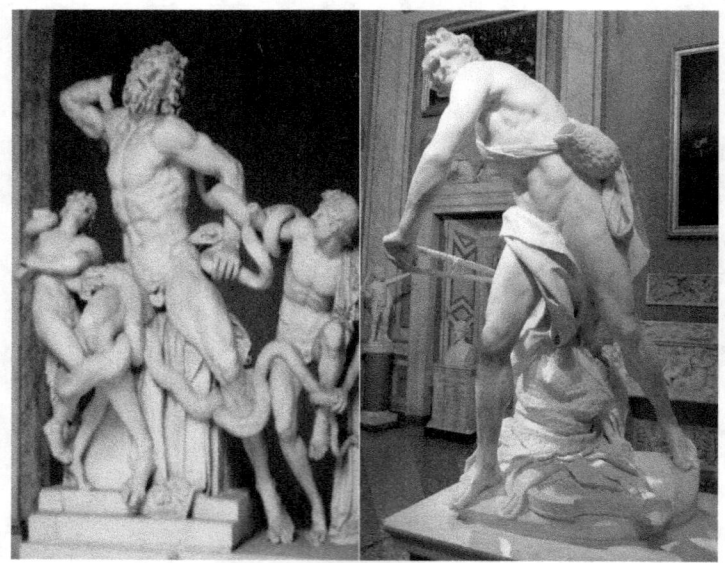

Photo credits: *David* (right) is taken by Sailko and is licensed under the Creative Commons Attribution 3.0 Unported license. *Laocoon* is taken by Michael Bausch.

We know he is confident his stone will hit the mark because if he misses he will trip over that which lies underneath. He knows he will not miss, so the clutter beneath him does not concern him.

Bernini and Michelangelo have carved the same figure, using the same medium, marble, and the same content, David engaging Goliath. Yet the iconology differs, the meaning of the piece. For Michelangelo, his *David* steps out to meet the new era that was later called the Renaissance, and Bernini's shows the ultra-confidence of the period called Baroque that invites the viewer into the emotional power of the church, and hence back into a confident faith.

Throughout my Italian journey, I saw other sculptures by Michelangelo that were calm, in repose, and on the verge of action, while Bernini's were all active, energetic, and freely in motion.

Unlike Bernini's *David*, where the invisible Goliath is felt in the Laocoon-type style of rippling and struggling muscles, Michelangelo's Goliath is in the eyes of *David*. He is, like Hercules, the "personification of physical strength" (19) and, like Apollo (p. 25), "standing for the rational and civilized side" of human nature. (20)

These qualities of strength, rationality, and civilization were qualities promoted by the Renaissance as its painters, sculptors, writers, thinkers, urban upper classes, and political dynasties helped forge a new outlook on life and Christian faith.

Through the eyes of his *David* Michelangelo helps us to see, rather than look, into this era of a renewed confidence in the power of humanity to join with God in a creative partnership.

Chapter 4

VENICE: INNOCENTS

La Strage Degli Innocenti (The Slaughter of the Innocents), Bonifacio Dei Pitati E Bottega, (Veronese 1487-1553 Venezia) Cat. N. 319. Oil on canvas, measurements not indicated, but I would say 54x81 inches. Gallerie della' Accademia, Venezia.

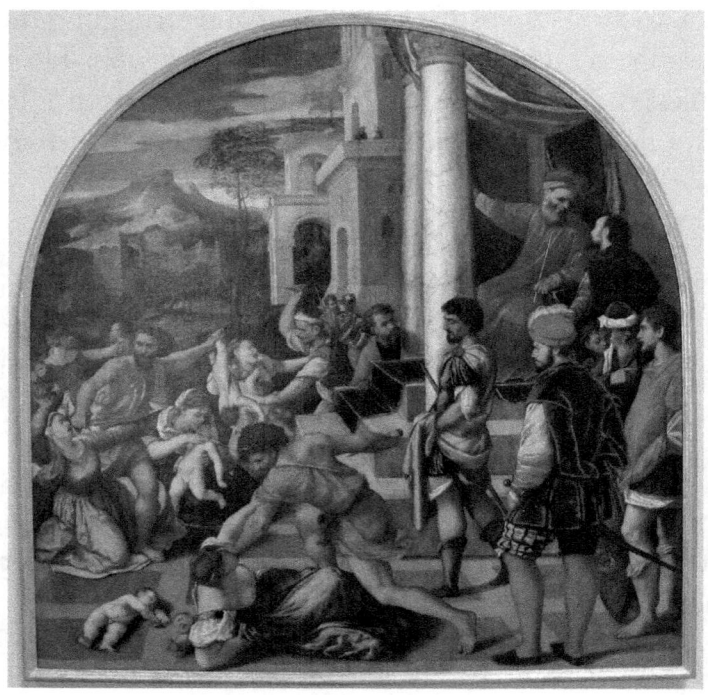

Photo credit: Used under the Creative Commons Attribution-Share Alike 3.0 Unported license.

I am always interested in portrayals of this most poignant episode from the nativity story, found only in Matthew's gospel, and in fact deleted from the common lectionary because the horrible content of the episode might just be too much for Christmas churchgoers looking for a cuddly baby story (Matt. 2: 16).

Because he feels threatened by the magi's report of the birth of a new Jewish king, Herod sends troops to Bethlehem to kill baby boys two years old and under. Joseph, warned in a dream, takes Mary and the infant Jesus into Egypt.

Innocents' Day is traditionally observed on December 28. Its modern parallels in December include the massacre at Wounded Knee in 1868 on December 28 and the Christmas bombings of North Vietnam in 1972, but the day includes remembering any killing of innocent children.

Of Raphael's six tapestries of the life of Christ in the long passageway of the Vatican Museum, three are devoted to the slaughter of the innocents. Horror and movement are all conveyed in the weaving. In the first tapestry, a mother pushes her hand into the face of a soldier, screaming at him as if to shout, "How can you do this?" while another mother cradles her wounded child.

In the second, a mother looks angrily at a soldier while her husband seems to ask, "What are you doing?" Meanwhile, a soldier mashes the head of an infant with his hand as he prepares to stab the child. In the third tapestry, a mother shields her baby with her body as the soldier has the boy by the leg.

In the final tapestry, Christ walks out of the tomb and the soldiers flee or fall away, proclaiming that while earlier in the slaughter of the innocents the powers of death are in control, now at the resurrection death and its agents have no power.

The slit in Christ's side is like that seen on a baby in the first tapestry, each a mirror image of the other. In these beautiful tapestries, Raphael provides a coherent theology of the nativity and the resurrection, even if the lectionary does not, another fine reason to include art in Protestant worship and education.

After standing in line for more than an hour to get into Florence's Accademia and Uffizi museums, it was a real pleasure to be able to walk into Venice's Accademia without a wait. Although small, this important gallery contains some of the finest works of the Venetian High Renaissance. This period of painting is marked by "bright colors, big canvases, Renaissance architectural settings, scenes of Venice life, and three-dimensional realism." (21)

To describe Bonifacio's *La Strage Degli Innocenti* I must begin with Giorgione's better-known *The Tempest*, as it is representative of Bonifacio's approach. (Unfortunately, Bonifacio's *La Strage* was pictured neither in the gallery catalogue nor in any nearby postcard.)

In *The Tempest*, we find a balanced Renaissance scene, with a mother quietly nursing her baby and a man standing across from her in a relaxed posture. In the center of the painting near the vanishing point is a bolt of lightning, a harbinger of the coming storm that will upset the balance, proportion, and calm of the scene.

A more familiar Bonifacio work, *Il Ricco Epulone (The Rich Man's Feast)*, develops a similar theme. A single large canvas, the artist uses pillars to separate the work into one central panel and two side panels. In the central panel, the lord and lady of a fine, stately manor are seated at table, looking melancholy and sharing a cup of wine. Before them at the table is a small group of young people, playing and listening to music. The manor and a lovely garden lane are in the background.

In the left panel behind the couple are various servants and attendants, chatting quietly and relaxing. In the right panel we find a different kind of energy. A beggar stoops forward, seeking alms. Two dogs lick at his legs. And in the top right corner of the canvas, above and behind the beggar, seemingly invisible to everyone, are red flames and a billowing of black smoke.

Like the lightning in *The Tempest*, this forest fire is threatening the serenity of the scene, this melancholy scene, for somehow in the faces of the rich there is an awareness of this approaching devastation, but an unwillingness or an inability to act.

I should add that while observing the painting, two young boys came rushing up, quickly counted the dogs they saw – four – and then disappeared again. They helped me notice a dog I had missed! It is in fact a small, white dog who seems to be looking in the fire's direction and recognizing the coming danger.

If you were to slice the canvas in a diagonal from top left to bottom right, the bottom triangle formed by the diagonal offers very little action, only a relaxed nonchalance, if not melancholy. In the upper triangle we see the action of the fire, the beggar, and the dogs. We shall see this structure in *La Strage*. Why the beggar? Is this a portrayal of Luke's story of the rich man and Lazarus (Luke 16:19-31)?

At least one art book says the title is *The Banquet of Dives* (22), the Accademia catalogue calls it *The Rich Epicure*, and another translation could be *The Rich Man's Feast*. Is the fire a premonition of the hell into which the rich man is cast in Luke's story? Is the black velvet over the head of the lord and lady painted to look like billowing black smoke over their heads?

As in many paintings, one small detail in the painting leads us into new worlds of interpretation: the lightning in Giorgone's *Tempest*, the keys in the Sistine's *The Giving Of The Keys To St. Peter*, the crumbling foot of the statue in Botticelli's *La Calunnia*, the fire in the corner of *The Rich Man's Feast*.

We finally arrive at *La Strage Degli Innocenti*. This particular painting caught my attention a year ago because as the killing happens the officers of the killers stand by with studied nonchalance and display a kind of seeing that is impervious to moral argument.

In contrast with David's calm and confident gaze and with Bernini's dove of spiritual authority (below), we find a portrayal of looking and not recognizing something evil at work, seeing and yet not seeing, of passionate killing and defending loved ones counterbalanced by a studied nonchalance and passivity.

As I observed other people as they approached and noticed the painting, it appeared to me that the eye is drawn to the writhing action in the bottom section of the canvas. It is a seething mass of women, babies, and men with knives who are grabbing and stabbing the children. Next, the eye goes to the top of the canvas, which portrays a beautiful distant natural scene of trees, mountains, and a placid city wall.

Moving down and right from there is a balanced Renaissance building, complete with columns, serving as backdrop to the adjacent canopy, beneath which sits a man looking off in the distance, in conversation with another. Other men stand around, leaning on pillars. A young boy rests his chin on the shoulder of an older man, and they are speaking and listening, turned away from the writhing mass next to them.

Like Michelangelo with *David*, Bonifacio divides the canvas diagonally. The shape of the canvas is the top half of an oval. Taking a line from the upper left and moving it down to the bottom right corner, one can see a harmonious layout: In the bottom sector there is agonized horror, while in the upper sector there are serenity, calm, even boredom.

The bottom section shows five mothers and four killers, two with knives and one with a sword. The scene is reminiscent of Raphael's tapestries: One mother holds her dead baby boy and screams in horror. Another mother watches as a killer holds her boy and has his sword drawn. Another boy clings to his mother's neck as he sees the sharp knife coming down toward him, while his mother tries to push the killer away, his hand grabbing the boy's leg.

On the floor beneath them lies one dead baby, while another next to him is shielded by his mother's body as the soldier/killer mashes her face with his left hand and begins to slash at the baby beneath her with his right.

In the upper section, by contrast, there is no hint of anything gone wrong. Groups of men are in quiet conversation; the man on the chair beneath the canopy is gesturing towards the mountains as if describing one of his hunting exploits.

29

The Renaissance building in the background is all pillars, order, and balance. The three men in the foreground are looking at something in the bottom section of the painting, and each has his hands in his pockets. One leans against a pillar, another against the picture frame, and still another stands looking calm and confident.

He stands like Paul in Fra Angelico's fresco *The Stoning of St. Stephen* (in the small chapel of Pope Nicholas V among the Raphael Rooms in the Vatican Museum), where Paul holds the cloaks of the executioners, watching dispassionately and standing erect with a posture that says, "This needs to happen."

Taken as a whole, the horror of the painting grows because the viewer notices the nonchalant men are watching the killing of the babies. The men stand, hands in pockets, relaxed, with expressions that betray the men's recognition that the slaughter goes well and they will not need to intervene.

Only the child leaning on the shoulder of the old man seems to notice something wrong, for he looks as if he is consciously avoiding looking at the scene taking place below him and to his right. He has a look of sadness on his face, as if only the child understands the true horror of what is taking place.

The man on the chair reminds us of the great hymn *Once To Every Man And Nation* in which James Russell Lowell writes, "Truth forever on the scaffold, wrong forever on the throne." (23)

They watch the scene as Cesare Borgia (1476-1507) is said to have responded to the violence he personally ordered: "Notorious for his nonchalance while witnessing murders, he once invited four high-ranking officers to a banquet and continued munching on a drumstick while they were strangled in front of him." (24)

Bonifacio seems to have painted a picture that, on the one hand, depicts Renaissance order, calm, and balance and, on the other, foretells a coming violence.

The men who wear red caps and robes seem to have more "blood" on them than the slaughtered babies in front of the men. Two crosses form a pattern in the floor. On one cross stand the three nonchalant soldiers, and on the other cross lie two babies and a mother.

The crucifiers and the crucified all claim the power of the cross. The light in the painting is evident in the sky behind the mountains in the background, the pillars supporting the nice building, and in the naked babies and faces of their mothers. The heavens look on as the Renaissance looks on, and life fades.

Further study with my own eye, in response to the question where does my eye go first, showed I am attracted to the bright white pillars. Then my eye goes down to the face of the man wearing the red hat, and I notice he is watching something with interest.

Then I see what he sees, the killing of these babies and the agony of their mothers as they frantically try to protect their babies with the mothers' own lives.

In real life approaching this scene, we would first hear it rather than see it. We would hear the cries and the screams and the gyrating bodies in struggle. Only later might we notice the nonchalance of the witnesses.

Bonifacio, as painter, helps us see this apathy in the face of suffering.

As I watched other people view the painting, they seemed to begin with the slaughter section, moved to the background, and then sometimes to the men standing as mute witnesses. Then these viewers often went to the title of the painting, discovered it was *The Slaughter of the Innocents* and then looked again at the slaughter scene to confirm they caught what the painting was about.

Yet, the painting may be less about the slaughter and more about the dispassionate viewers. Unlike Bernini's dove, which we view from below and from a distance to present us with a sense of awestruck wonder, or Michelangelo's *David*, also viewed from below and meant to be viewed from a distance as an image of strength and divine/human partnership, Bonifacio has us view the scene at ground level and from only a slight distance of a few feet.

How do we respond to this scene? Are we forever powerless in the face of such slaughter, unable to intercede, invited in only as an observer who cannot change the scene? Are we motivated to prevent such slaughters or to intervene when they happen in our day? Only the day before I noticed a newspaper photograph of Rwandan children lying sick and dying in a refugee camp. I felt this to be an ugly, horrible scene and an intrusion into my wonderful vacation touring art museums.

The slaughter of the innocents continues in our day and time, and once again we are invited to choose how we shall participate in it: to protect the innocent in a futile freneticism, to be the innocent in the grip of the killer, to use our strength to kill, to stand idly by and simply watch, to talk about other things in the midst of killing, to view and then to walk away, to somehow learn to prevent such slaughters?

Even as Tillich gained new confidence and hope after World War I by "one moment of beauty" with Botticelli's *Madonna and Child With Singing Angels*, he would later suggest that Renaissance art is not religious because there are too much harmony and balance and not enough suggestion of the dark side of existence. (25) I wonder if he would change his view were he to have noticed *La Strage*. He has defined a work like this to be "explicitly religious if it expresses the artist's sensitive and honest search for ultimate meaning and significance with the aid of a recognizable religious subject matter . . . ." (26)

It is clear Bonifacio uses a religious subject – not only by the content of men killing babies, but clearly in the selected title of the work – and that the contrasting scene of studied nonchalance in the face of horror raises the question, "What's wrong with this picture?"

Perhaps it is because of this question and the dark side present in Bonifacio's painting that I had been drawn to it and found it important enough to include as one of my focus pieces of art.

Chapter 5

ROME: ST. PETER'S CHAIR

THE CATHEDRA PETRI 1656-66, Bernini, gilt stucco, marble, bronze, stained glass, The Apse of St. Peter's Basilica, Rome.

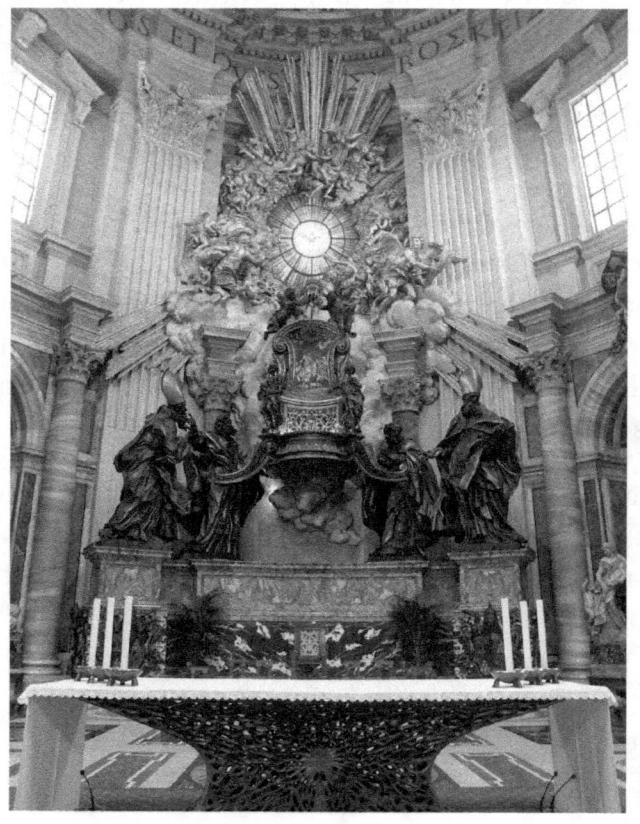

Of all the times of day to visit St. Peter's Square, perhaps the loveliest is near midnight on a warm summer's night. The tourists are all gone, and all that linger are a few young couples and a car or two of *polizia.*

Beneath the full moon and the gentle quiet of the night, one can look at the ancient obelisk and ponder how on a night much like this one the Romans used to race their chariots on this site and burn people as human torches to light the sky.

Not far from this spot, Peter was said to have been crucified, upside down, and buried along with other martyrs in the cemetery just near the circus. Constantine built a basilica on the site (324 A.D.), over the burial place of Peter, and this basilica was later rebuilt in its present form (1506-1626). (27)

Michelangelo intended to use the more egalitarian Greek cross floor plan, but that was changed to the Latin cross plan to emphasize the grandeur of the building and its identification with the crucifixion and martyrdoms of Jesus and Peter.

While one of the chapels in the basilica marks the traditional spot of Peter's burial, it is the *Cathedra Petri* that catches my attention. Bernini used stucco, wood, stained glass, and marble in his mixed-media presentation of the *Cathedra. Cathedra* is the Latin rendering of the Greek word *cathizo*, or seat. It is the seat or chair representing the teaching authority of the church.

Using a typical Renaissance sense of balance and proportion, as seen in the columns of the elliptical St. Peter's "square," Bernini lined up the high altar, the stained- glass dove, and the obelisk in the center of the ellipse outside. It was at first my supposition that Bernini lined up the dove and the obelisk.

On the first morning we were present in the square, I could see the obelisk aligned with the central door into the basilica. It wasn't until Sunday morning, when the central door is opened, that I could stand inside the basilica, face the center of the cross over the baldacchino and the dove behind it, and then turn around and look out of the center door to see the obelisk looming in the sun with its tiny cross on the top – from dove to cross a perfect centering.

Drawn into the basilica by the elliptical colonnade, looking from above like the "arms of the church," we are aware that each step along the way is "almost a succession of tableaux" and that we are a part of a grand design whose purpose is "eloquent praise of the Church Triumphant." (28)

When I enter the church I am struck with the immensity of the facility, the small scale of humanity when compared to the huge sanctuary, and then drawn to the golden light coming from the small orb at the center of the apse several hundred yards ahead.

The *Cathedra* itself is surrounded by rays of light that radiate from the stained glass dove, representing the Holy Spirit. Angels cling to the rays and are in various states of motion, some hanging on for dear life while others are looking toward the dove. Most books suggest that the *Cathedra* is held in place by the figures of four fathers of the church, Ambrose, Augustine, Athanasias, and John Chrysostom. (29)

My impression is that the *Cathedra* is floating out of the heavens and that while the four figures of the church appear to support the church with their strength, they in fact seem to simply stabilize the chair. A closer scrutiny, impossible for this observer, might show their hands holding the chair, but my view was that no hand held the chair, except by the slightest of touches.

Iconologically then, the four fathers stabilize, support, and respect this chair come from heaven, representing the teaching of the church through the bishop of Rome. Bernini carves his figures in motion, and even though their bodies are hidden by flowing robes, you can still see the outlines of the bodies beneath the marble "fabric."

Typical of Bernini is the representation of the divine in the physical. In his *Transverberation of St. Theresa* in Santa Maria della Vittoria in Rome, we see her body in the midst of her mystical experience, floating on clouds of light, in a sweet ecstasy. In this "peerless jewel . . . one of the noblest sculptures of all time" (from a historical description of the church interior provided by the church of Santa Maria della Vittoria), Bernini uses "the skill of the experienced impresario."

The statue is set in such a way that the angel and the saint appear to be part of an apparition, floating, framed by a stage like proscenium, with a burst of light flooding down golden shafts from what seems an opening in the heavens above.

The artist's intention is to create an environment in which the barriers between the beholder and the work of art may vanish, and we may experience it subjectively, knowing what Francis of Sales called "the soul's liquefaction." (30)

It is the intention of such art to represent "the saints as visionaries, at the moment when the barriers between reality and the supernatural are transcended." (31)

It is the Council of Trent (completed 1563) and its teaching of transubstantiation, that is, the wine and bread actually become Christ's body, that presents Bernini with the opportunity to portray the physical details of a human figure, because now divinity in the flesh is legitimately portrayed in bread and wine – and in marble as well. (32)

In the *Cathedra Petri* biblical references to the work of the Holy Spirit are translated through the artist's vision. The Spirit-dove, present at the baptism of Jesus and at the transfiguration, accompanies the heavenly voice that declares, "This is my beloved son with whom I am well pleased. Listen to him." (Matt.17:5)

The declared imperative is implied in the dove's presence over the *Cathedra*, the teaching seat of the church. This is an important symbol during the time of the Counter-Reformation, when Protestant teachings must be engaged and defeated.

The dove itself seems to be in a soaring position, wings outstretched, perfectly and harmoniously balanced in the window. I observed doves from my window in a high area of the central town of Siena and noticed how they soared effortlessly below me.

Bernini's *Cathedra* shows movement in everything except the chair and the dove: The Renaissance placid calm is represented even as the baroque spiritual ecstasy surrounds those portrayals.

The angels, heavenly clouds, gilded rays of light, and the *Cathedra* coming out of it beneath the soaring supervision of the dove present an inspiring look at a creative process. The imagery need not be dismissed by the Protestant mind, for it could understand the symbolism of the *Cathedra* as the authority of the teachings revealed by the creative power of the Holy Spirit.

This way of understanding the symbolism represents a more universal *cathedra* rather than a narrow, papal *cathedra*. The dove provides balance, stability, and peace in the midst of all the gilded movement surrounding it.

Just as the Spirit-dove creates with a burst of light over chaos (see Genesis 1:1-3), so does the triumph of the *Cathedra* emerge out of the chaos of the Roman circus and the crucifixion of Peter.

To the Protestant mind, this arrangement of materials speaks less of the authority of the pope and more about the simple greatness of the fisherman from the northern shore of Galilee.

Another view might be to simply ignore the *Cathedra*, the bishops who hold it, the angels, and clouds and focus instead upon the unity of the dove in the apse and the obelisk in the center of the ellipse outside.

The great welcoming arms of the colonnade draw us into the sanctuary, whose singular, quiet focus is the piercing vision of the dove. The keys, held by angels over the chair, represent Peter's receiving them from Jesus.

They unlock the mysteries of God and become the primary symbol of the power of teaching, distinguished from the obelisk they face that symbolizes the imperial Roman oppression, the hideous spectacle of the circus, and the silent witness over the terrible deaths of the expendables of Roman society.

The cross, seated as it is upon the top of the obelisk, is a reminder that the Christian story now takes precedence over

– and redeems – the Egyptian/Roman imperial saga.

Bernini's grand vision creates in the viewer a sense of awe and beauty and offers creative refreshment to those who linger in its light.

Chapter 6

ROME: CARAVAGGIO

Calling of St. Matthew, 1599-1600, Carravaggio, Oil on canvas, measurements 127x130 inches, Contarelli Chapel, San Luigi dei Francesi, Rome.

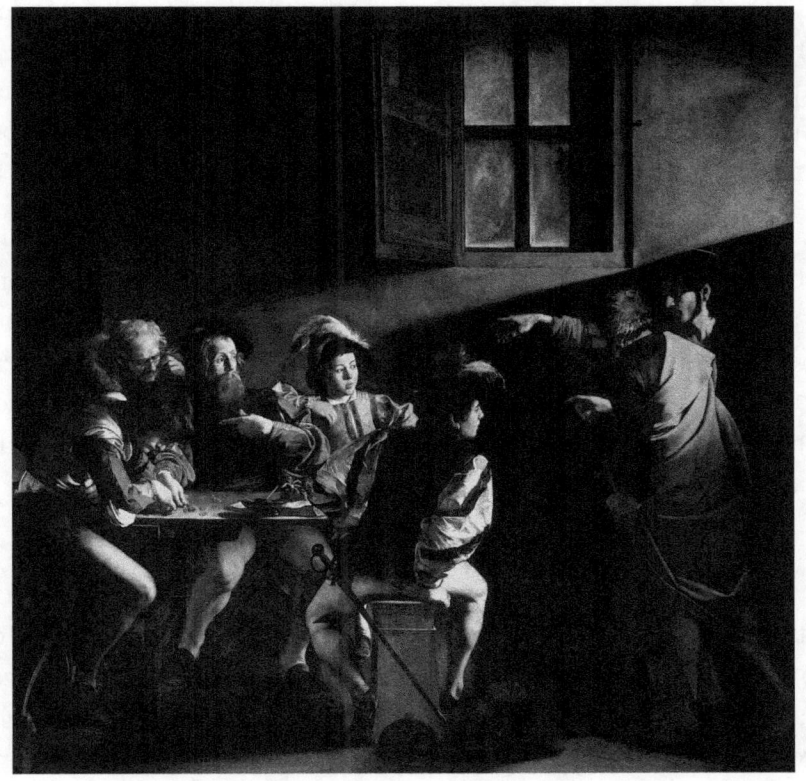

Photo credit: This is a faithful photographic reproduction of a two-dimensional, public domain work of art.

In June 1995, I led a small group of pilgrims to Rome and the Vatican to experience a sampling of the religious art and architecture offered there. During that trip I had a few moments alone with Caravaggio's painting. Returning home, I have been able to reflect upon that work more completely through the use of three of Doug Adams' books, *Art As Religious Studies* (1987), *Transcendence With the Human Body in Art* (1991*)*, and *Eyes to See Wholeness* (1995).

Five ideas provide a springboard for my reflections on the painting:

1) "A viewer's experiences, attitudes, and expectations affect what is seen or experienced in any artwork. As expectations vary from day to day, the same person may experience and evaluate an artwork differently at different times." (*Transcendence With the Human Body in Art,* p.130-131).

2) The richness of religious art is partly a result of an artist's portrayal of the entire biblical story rather than one single, small feature. "The biblical story should be seen fully and not heard partially. Since visual art may present simultaneously a number of separate events or ideas, such images are able to give us a sense of wholeness while readings often give us only a part." (*Eyes to See Wholeness*, p. 1).

3) The veiling and unveiling of a work, as in Christo's art, reminds us of the interplay of light and darkness, of covered and uncovered, of the value of different experiences that reveal more in a work of art. I have found squinting the eyes while looking at a painting will often reveal more, as one is able to notice forms and structures in the dimness that are often blocked by fuller light. (*Transcendence With the Human Body in Art*).

4) "To be trained in the discipline of seeing involves the total engagement of the viewer, and the viewer in turn is

transformed." (*Art As Religious Studies*, p. 5)

5) "This kinesthetic method helps many students see in a painting or sculpture the details they miss when just looking. This method helps the viewers remember similar body shapes and gestures they have experienced in other works of art as well as in daily life." (Ibid., p. 200-201)

Each of these five ideas provides me a way to describe more fully my experience with Caravaggio's painting. At various points in this paper I will refer to the above five ideas as they have informed my seeing.

Before telling the particular story of my encounter with *Calling of St. Matthew*, I should first explain something about previous experiences with Caravaggio's work.

I have experienced Caravaggio's paintings at Santa Maria del Popolo and Santa Luigi dei Francesi in Rome three times, and each experience has offered me unexpected surprise.

On my first visit to Santa Maria del Popolo, I noticed a small group of people in a chapel. As I approached, I saw they were absorbed in the paintings on the wall. Noting the people to be from the United States, I asked, "What are we seeing here?"

They showed me the two paintings on the wall, *Crucifixion of St. Peter* and *Conversion on the Way to Damascus*. The women marveled at how these famous paintings were so accessible – and so fragile in that location with the afternoon sun shining upon them.

I was immediately attracted to *Crucifixion of St. Peter* because of the way Caravaggio captured a calm, serene look on Peter's face as his pierced body is awkwardly raised upside down on the cross. His executioners are shown in a state of confusion and discomfort as they try to raise the martyr. Caravaggio portrays the executioners' human struggle in counterpoint to the peaceful look of resolve on Peter's face.

This was my introduction to Caravaggio, and the beginning of a fascination with his use of light and darkness in his canvases.

On another visit to Rome, I was again treated to a surprising view of Caravaggio's work. This time I gained a lesson in perspective.

The night before, we had visited Piazza Navona, and I had stopped into a record store and discovered it to be the perfect place to find gifts for my daughters. Being without my money, however, I asked in Italian if the store would be open in the morning and found the business would be at 9 o'clock.

Early the next morning I returned and waited for the store to open. I strolled around the piazza and studied Bernini's fountain and the obelisk raised above the fountain. As 9 o'clock came and went, I realized the store had not opened. I wondered if I had gotten the time wrong – maybe I didn't catch the clerk saying "nuovo mezzo," or 9:30.

Knowing the church of San Luigi dei Francesi was nearby, I decided to visit my old friend Caravaggio while waiting for the store to open.

Entering the church, I was pleasantly surprised to find I was the only person there. I strolled to the chapel where Caravaggio had set three canvases, *Calling of St. Matthew, St. Matthew and the Angel,* and *Martyrdom of St. Matthew.*

The chapel was darker than I expected, and at first the dark canvases were barely visible to my eyes. I had no coins for the coin-operated lights that would illuminate the paintings. I was disappointed, yet decided to stay and see what I could see.

Concentrating on *Calling of St. Matthew*, I began to see things I hadn't seen before in a previous visit – the darkness revealed new details, and as my eyes grew accustomed to the darkness, even more stood out.

This echoed something Doug Adams had written, "A viewer's experiences, attitudes, and expectations affect what is seen or experienced in any artwork. As expectations vary from day to day, the same person may experience and evaluate an artwork differently at different times." (*Transcendence With the Human Body in Art* [p.130-131]).

In the dark, for example, I noticed the window above the hand of Christ and saw for the first time the cross in the window and how the line of the cross extended down to Christ's hand.

I could see the diagonal of light/darkness that extends downward from the top right to the bottom left of the canvas and how the brightest face is that of the young attendant to Matthew's left. Matthew's face is next brightest, and third brightest is the man leaning over Matthew's right shoulder.

In the darkness I could see the boy's face shining, and in that light I wondered: Was this boy the center of the painting, and not St. Matthew? Wasn't it Matthew who wrote, "Except as ye become like little children, you will not enter the kingdom of heaven"? (Matthew 19:14)

45

The dim light was changing my perspective and opening up new interpretations of Caravaggio's great painting. ("The biblical story should be seen fully and not heard partially. Since visual art may present simultaneously a number of separate events or ideas, such images are able to give us a sense of wholeness while readings often give us only a part." [*Eyes to See Wholeness, p. 1*]).

Next, I saw a "diagonal of hands" – first the hand of Christ pointing toward Matthew, then Matthew's hand clearly pointing to himself (a detail I had missed during all previous viewings, as the finger appears to point to the man hunched over on his right. In the darkness the finger more clearly points inward toward Matthew's body). Extending down from Matthew's hand are the other hands on the table, counting the money.

This "diagonal of hands" reveals a central theme. Between the appointing hand of Christ and the money-counting hands on the table is the questioning hand – is it me you are pointing to?

Matthew is seen at the moment of decision regarding God or mammon – his right hand is on the money on the table while his left points to himself. Between God and mammon is the choice – which one will it be? "No one can serve two masters; for either he will hate the one and love the other, or he will be devoted to one and despise the other. You cannot serve God and mammon." (Matthew 6:24)

There also seem to be a diagonal of darkness and a diagonal of light. From the upper right, through the hat of the boy, and to the head of the man completely engrossed in his counting is the dark diagonal. From the center left to the middle right is the diagonal of light, culminating in the boy's face.

Only by seeing this painting in the dim light could I detect these diagonals.

"The veiling and unveiling of a work, as in Christo's art, reminds us of the interplay of light and darkness, of covered and uncovered, of the value of different experiences that reveal more in a work of art. (*Transcendence With the Human Body in Art*).

I have found squinting the eyes while looking at a painting will often reveal more, as one is able to notice forms and structures in the dimness that are often blocked by fuller light."

After thrilling to the new details emerging in the different light, it was time to get back to the record store.

I left the church and went back to Piazza Navona and realized the store still was not open. Yet in that instant I had that flash of "Aha!" The new perspective gained from the chapel at S. Luigi dei Francesi opened my mind enough to realize – recognize – I had been waiting in front of the wrong store. I was at the opposite end of the square from where I was the previous night!

The store was where it should be and had opened at 9 a.m. I just had entered the piazza from a different direction and was waiting in the wrong place.

Just as the darkness in the church led to new understanding, so did that experience open me to realize I'd reversed my perspective in the piazza.

47

As the revelations in the darkness changed my view of this painting, so did that change in perspective open me to realizing I needed a new perspective in order to find that record store! ("To be trained in the discipline of seeing involves the total engagement of the viewer, and the viewer in turn is transformed." [*Art As Religious Studies*, p. 5]).

Over the following weeks, I studied this painting further and found that in the fuller light of reproductions there is yet more to see.

In fact, one might find at least 10 scripture passages from Matthew's Gospel, all "quoted" in the painting's imagery. While the painting illustrates the obvious scriptural calling of St. Matthew, "As Jesus passed on from there, he saw a man called Matthew sitting at the tax office; and he said to him, 'Follow me.' And he rose and followed him." (Matthew 9:9), other passages are illustrated:

The boy sitting to Matthew's left, central in the picture, and with the most lit face (Matthew 5:10 "Let your light shine before men, that they may see your good works and glorify your Father in heaven . . .), may well be Caravaggio's illustration of "Except as ye become like little children ye shall not enter the kingdom of heaven." (Matthew 19:14)

Could it be that the boy will come along with Matthew, or at least have his life changed at some later date by the One who is calling Matthew in that moment?

The sword in the bottom center of the painting could well be illustrating both Matthew's martyrdom (depicted on the opposite wall from this painting) and Jesus' statement in Matthew 10:34, "I have not come to bring peace, but a sword."

The inkwell, pen, and book on the table, used to record the taxes, will take on a new function as Matthew takes up this book in the service of the Gospel and begins to record the acts of God, not the accumulations of mammon. "Do not lay up for yourselves treasures on earth . . . but lay up for yourselves treasure in heaven . . . ."(Matthew 6:19)

The cross in the window and the sword by the soldier's side both illustrate Matthew 10:38-39, "He who does not take his cross and follow me is not worthy of me. He who finds his life will lose it, and he who loses his life for my sake will find it." In the calling of Matthew the cross is revealed in the flung-open window cover. Calling and cross are dynamically linked.

As the Christ with halo calls the Matthew with a hat, we get the impression Matthew will soon give up his hat of the tax collector for the halo of martyrdom.

The two sets of visible eyes, on the lit faces of Matthew and the boy next to him, show Matthew 6:22, "The eye is the lamp of the body. So, If your eye is sound, your whole body will be full of light." Likewise, the man to Matthew's right, engrossed in the money counting, needs to struggle with eyeglasses in order to see – his eye is not sound, focused as it is on mammon.

The light upon the central faces comes from Christ, "I am the light of the world." (John 8:12)

Other details emerge. It is very hard to make out table legs – it appears the table is supported by human legs – this commitment to mammon is supported by human choice, and when enough legs abandon that table and follow Christ, the folly of choosing mammon will be seen.

The feather in the boy's hat points towards Matthew's finger, while the feather in the other guard's hat points to Peter's finger. Notice Peter's finger in imitation of Christ's appointing finger – Peter, looking tentative, in the early moments of his own calling.

Notice, too, the walking stick he holds in his left hand. After all twelve disciples are called, in Matthew 10:9, Jesus assembles them and tells them, "Take no gold . . . no bag for your journey, or two tunics, or sandals, or a staff . . . ."

Just as Matthew's life is changing, so will Peter's life continue to change – he's given up his fishing, and next he'll have to give up his staff – such continual change is a part of life with Christ.

Notice Jesus' hand. I wonder if a better title for the painting is "The Appointment of Matthew." There are no words suggesting a "calling" in this silent portrayal, as the calling is made by the silent, pointing finger. "He stretched out his hand and touched him . . . ." (Matthew 8:3)

It is here, at the hand of Christ, where we might employ the kinesthetic method of interpretation. Where have we seen that hand before? Isn't it the same hand that Michelangelo painted onto the Sistine ceiling the hand of God creating Adam?

By taking Michelangelo's God-hand and putting it on his Christ, Caravaggio is reminding us of Paul's interpretation of the nature of Christ in his letter to the Colossians, 1:15-25:

"He is the image of the invisible God, the firstborn of all creation; for in him all things in heaven and on earth were created . . . all things have been created through him and for him. He is the head of the body, the church; he is the beginning, the firstborn from the dead . . . . For in him all the fullness of God was pleased to dwell and through him God was pleased to reconcile to himself all things, whether on earth or in heaven, by making peace through the blood of his cross."

Christ is the new Adam (the hand), the fullness of God (the halo), bringing reconciliation (the calling of Matthew) to all things by the cross (the window). This is fun! ("This kinesthetic method helps many students see in a painting or sculpture the details they miss when just looking. This method helps the viewers remember similar body shapes and gestures they have experienced in other works of art as well as in daily life." [Ibid., p. 200-201].)

Finally, some thoughts about frontality. While Matthew's body is facing the viewer and Matthew's upper body is leaning backwards, his legs seem ready to spring forward into action. Christ's body is facing the viewer as well.

Trying his pose with our own bodies, noticing his right foot planted firmly facing the viewer, we realize he faces us and not Matthew. He is both ready to move out the door from which he had come in – here is a man of action and movement – and he is ready to face us, the viewers, as he turns to leave.

I can see him looking me in the eye and extending his hand to me or to any of us viewing this picture. I can see Matthew, in the next instant, facing the viewer frontally and looking to see our response to the same call. We know what happened to both Jesus and Matthew. They seem to be ready to watch our response to their story.

A chance moment with a painting, themes revealed in the darkness, a lesson in perspective, and seeing illuminated by concentrated if not practiced viewing – all combine to provide a creative encounter whose lessons will inform my understanding of art and Gospel.

Author's note: Over the years I have preached this painting by projecting it on a screen for all to see and have taught with the painting in a university course in New Testament studies.

One detail pointed out by other observers is that the costumes of Caravaggio's characters seem to be from the artist's time in early 17th-century Rome (He was known to use his friends and other acquaintances as models for his figures), and the clothing worn by Peter and Jesus suggests a 1st-century time period. This does show how the old story is also a new story.

Other observers point out the need to also notice all the characters are white – and male – and that while the painting seems to exclude others, our interpretations of the painting may and must certainly extend beyond maleness and whiteness.

Chapter 7

SAINT OBELISK

One of the sacred spaces of Christendom is St. Peter's Square in Rome. The elliptical "square" has been designed to welcome visitors and to draw them towards the basilica.

Standing as a focal point is an Egyptian obelisk that has been present in that area since 40 C.E. when Caligula had it placed in the center of his private chariot racetrack.

As already mentioned in Chapter 5, tradition says the obelisk bore silent witness to Peter's crucifixion and the deaths of others killed by Nero's purge of Christians and other scapegoats after the fire of Rome around 64 C.E.

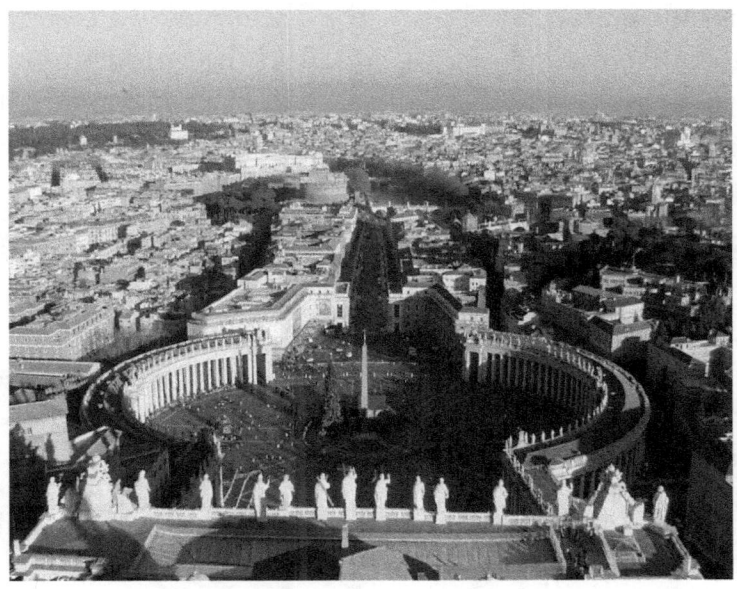

Photo credit: Michael Bausch

Because the obelisk is associated with these martyrdoms and its location now in the center of St. Peter's, I playfully call this chapter "Saint Obelisk." The Italian *santo* or "saint" simply means "holy." As we shall see, there is a holiness to the place this particular obelisk holds and the events that transpired beneath it so long ago.

Part 1: The Story of This Obelisk

Egyptian obelisks are thin, tapered four-sided pillars hewn from single blocks of granite quarried in the Aswan region of Upper Egypt. Weighing hundreds of tons and as tall as ninety feet, these monuments were transported to temples and tombs throughout Egypt during the time of the pharaonic dynasties.

Many of these obelisks were inscribed with tales of pharaonic conquests. Today, the obelisk at St. Peter's is one of 13 in Rome and one of 30 left in the world. Egypt has eight obelisks, the UK has four, and France, Israel, Turkey, Poland, and the U.S. each have one.

For a long time, what is now St. Peter's Square and Basilica was actually a racetrack, called a "circus." It is said Caligula used this particular track for his private chariot practice. By the time of Nero, some 20 years later, the track had become like the other Roman circuses, not only a racetrack for horses and horse-drawn chariots but a venue for spectacles such as mortal combat.

Left standing in the same area at the Vatican Hill for nearly 2,000 years, the 83-foot Vatican obelisk now serves as a memorial to the martyrdom of Christians, including Peter, who died at the circus during "entertainment" in the reign of Nero around 64-66 C.E.

Tradition says Peter was crucified near this obelisk and buried in an adjacent cemetery. The Basilica of St. Peter's, first built by Constantine in 324 and rebuilt during the 15-17th centuries, stands over what is thought to be Peter's tomb.

This particular obelisk stands as a still, mute witness to the mystery of the faith of Jesus, Peter, and unnamed men and women, in whose memory Christians gather when remembering their sacred history.

I first visited St. Peter's Square in 1993 and was immediately struck with the immensity of the architecture of the square and basilica. During a midnight visit to a square empty of its tourists, I was moved to remember the event that lay behind the architectural beauty, the martyrdom of Peter of Galilee in the Roman capital.

Remembering his martyrdom, his witness, I became aware that at this spot a Galilean fisherman who walked beside Jesus of Nazareth died in testimony to the Risen Christ.

In another visit in 1994, after learning more about the particular choice of this site for St. Peter's Basilica, I became more deeply aware of the masterful architecture which sought to communicate the glory of Christian faith.

After mass on a Sunday morning, the center doors of the basilica opened outward to reveal a view of the obelisk from within the basilica. I could see that the obelisk was lined up with the stained-glass dove above the *Cathedra Petri* in the central apse.

I understood the artistic vision connecting the basilica with the obelisk, as the stained-glass dove of the Holy Spirit focused its gaze upon the Christian cross placed atop the obelisk. I knew the invigoration of spiritual and theological insight as I interpreted the cross over the obelisk to be a symbol of redemption over the chaos of imperial Egypt and Rome.

In January 1995, I was able to visit St. Peter's again, and this time I was surprised to see Christmas decorations added to the obelisk. At its base was a life-sized creche, complete with Mary, Joseph, magi, animals, plants indigenous to Israel-Palestine (olive, cactus, palm), and recorded Christmas music.

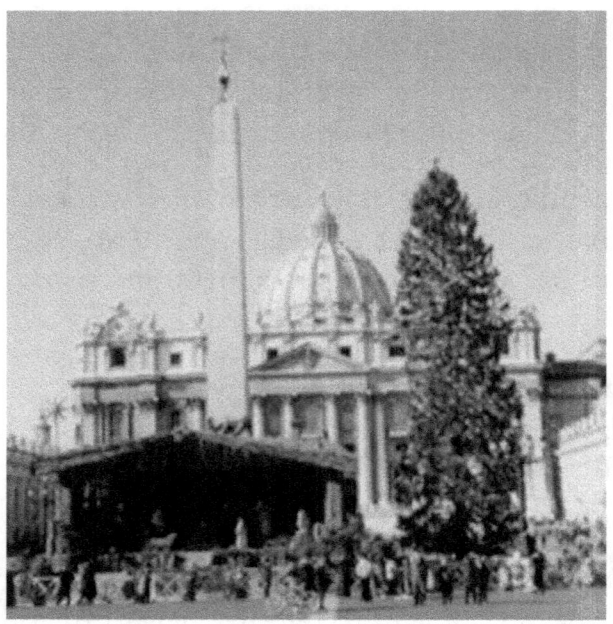

Photo credit: Michael Bausch

To the right of this scene was a huge decorated Christmas tree, whose ornaments shone in the sun and swayed in the stiff winter breeze.

This soft and gentle scene was a stark contrast to the scene beneath that obelisk some 1,930 years before, when the horrible events of Nero's retribution upon Christians in Rome forever sealed the obelisk's role as a memorial to their martyrdom.

It is thought that originally the Egyptian obelisks were tributes to the leadership of the pharaoh in whose honor a stone was erected. Most, if not all, probably had gold, silver, or other metallic alloys fixed to the triangular cap of the obelisk. This served to reflect the sun's rays.

Some obelisks were placed in pairs near the entrances of temples, one on the east side and the other on the west side, so as to reflect the rays of both the rising and setting sun.

Remembering that some of these stones were crafted and transported nearly 5,000 years ago, they represent the impressive artistic, engineering, and organizational talents of the Egyptian people, not to mention the ideological and religious fervor that made the whole enterprise important.

Egyptologists tend to agree that the obelisks were part of the sun worship that characterized Egyptian religious and political life. The thin obelisk seemed as an individual sun ray, especially as it reflected sunlight from the top.

"When inscribed with the name of the dedicator and placed in front of tombs and temples . . . the solar animation of the obelisk was . . . directly transferred to the person whose dedication it carried, calling him to life and making him partake in the eternal cycle of daily rebirth and revival." (1)

Others suggest that the obelisk is a great phallic symbol, taken from the Egyptian concept that the triangular top, or "benben," was thought to be "the petrified remains of the seed issued from the god at his first emission." (2)

Either phallus or sun's ray, the meaning for the Egyptians was the same: The obelisk represented the regeneration of life experienced each day as the sun set and rose again.

A great number of uninscribed obelisks were raised in Heliopolis, the city of the sun, and this cluster of pillars was associated with the largest library in the ancient world (later transferred to Alexandria), a university, and the Temple of the Sun. (3)

Centuries later, when Egypt was incorporated into the Roman empire in 30 B.C., we witness Roman interest in the obelisk. In recognition of the Roman annexation, Octavian ordered a "Forum Julium" to be laid out in Alexandria, complete with one of the obelisks from Heliopolis. This obelisk (83 feet high, 326 tons [4]) would later be taken to Caligula's circus in Rome, but more on that later. (5)

In 10 B.C. Augustus had the first Egyptian obelisk transported to Rome to be erected in the Circus Maximus. In his study of the Roman circuses, John Humphrey details the political reasons for the removal of this obelisk and its incorporation into the circus: It symbolized Augustus' new territory, available through his victory over Antony and Cleopatra; it arrived at a time when Romans were interested in Egyptian art and antiquities; and it served as "a spectacular way to assert one's power," "an impressive symbol of the ruler's power." (6)

Indeed, Augustus had inscriptions added to the faces of the obelisk to proclaim that "Egypt had been brought back into the power of the Roman people and that he himself 'had dedicated the obelisk to the Sun as a gift.'" (7)

Augustus deliberately associated his personal power with that of the sun, the circus, and the temple to the sun built at the circus:

"The dedication to the Sun makes full sense when we restore the Temple of the Sun as presiding over the finish (line) . . . . For in a building which was already dedicated to the Sun, what could be a better gift than an obelisk, the symbol par excellence of Egyptian sun-worship? Augustus was deliberately reinforcing the ancient connection of sol with the Circus. According to Tertullian some said that the first circus spectacle was produced by Circe (daughter of the Sun) in honour of her father the Sun . . . (who is) the supreme charioteer." (8)

Iversen and others agree that Caligula brought the Vatican obelisk to Rome during his reign in 37-41 and had it placed in the Vatican circus, originally built for his personal chariot practice.

According to Dibner, the boat that transported the obelisk from Alexandria to Rome had "300 rowers and a ballast of 1,000 tons of grain, placed in sacks and fitted around the obelisk to keep it from shifting when the vessel rolled." (9) Caligula had this obelisk inscribed with a dedication to "the god Augustus, son of the god Julius, and to the god Tiberius, son of the god Augustus." (10)

Starting with Augustus, it became the Roman practice to place the obelisk on the "spina" of the circus, the barrier in the center of the elliptical race course. The "spina," or spine, was wide enough to hold shrines and statues and in itself was symbolic.

A sixth century historian says, "The spina represents the lot of the unhappy captives inasmuch as the Roman generals, marching over the backs of their enemies, reaped that joy which was the reward of their labours." (11)

The spina was decorated with statues of prisoners and other trophy monuments. Further, the word "spina" meant "thorn" or "spine" and hence the "barrier had come by then to symbolize the prickly fate and/or the broken spines of Rome's enemies." (12)

The Roman circus provided entertainment for Roman citizens in the form of horse races, chariot races, hunting events, and mortal combat. Captured enemies and condemned criminals would be trained for gladiatorial combat.

According to Tacitus, a Roman senator and historian in the first century, these " . . . games occupied 80 days a year . . . (and) were considered acts of religious cult. They were made up of races in the circuses, gladiatorial combat, bloody battles with beasts, naval battles, theatrical presentations, literary and musical competitions." (13)

Ancient graffiti record the fact that "cruciarii," or people sentenced to crucifixion, would also be part of the entertainment. (For a vivid description of the violent character of the "games," see Will Durant, Caesar and Christ, pp. 386-387.) (14)

In 64 C.E. during Nero's reign a fire that broke out in the Circus Maximus spread and destroyed much of Rome. Following the fire, Nero's games were "given an expiatory character . . . to placate the gods after the fatal fire." (15)

Tacitus says that Caligula's circus "witnessed the mass executions of Christians condemned to death by Nero after the fire of Rome in C.E. 64, culminating in the martyrdom of the Apostle Peter." (16) Among the truly terrible killing methods was . . . wrapping men in the skins of beasts so that they might be torn to pieces by the dogs, others were nailed to crosses or condemned to be burned alive, serving as torches to illuminate the darkness at the end of the day. (17)

A sixth century biographer records that Peter was crucified, most likely on the "spina" of the circus, and "buried on the Via Aurelia, alongside the circus of Nero in the Vatican near the area called 'Trionfale,' in the area where he was crucified the 29th of June." (18)

Iversen reminds us of the association of these events with the obelisk on the circus "spina."

"In the early history of the Church the death of the Apostle was an epoch-making event, and the area around the circus where his crucifixion had taken place 'close to the obelisk of Nero' became hallowed ground . . . ." (19)

During the second and third centuries a cemetery was developed in this vicinity, and excavations beneath St. Peter's have been able to determine the locations of various tombs in addition to remains of the circus structures.

In 324 Constantine built the first Christian church in Rome on the site of Peter's tomb and partially over ruins of the old circus. The obelisk, all that remained of the spina's symbols, stood just outside the sacristy.

Over time every other obelisk in Rome was broken and buried in the debris of the centuries, but it was only the obelisk at St. Peter's that stood intact, most probably because of its association with the Christian martyrdoms at that site.

By the 15th century, with the stabilizing of the church, various popes laid plans to restore both public and religious buildings and to rebuild Rome into the capital of Christendom. Under Pope Nicholas V (1447-55), plans were developed to move the obelisk some 275 yards from its position near the sacristy to the center of St. Peter's Square.

There it would be supported by four large bronze statues of the Evangelists and topped with "a bronze Jesus with a golden cross in his hand 'to strengthen the weak faith of the people by the greatness of that which it sees.'" (20)

But it wasn't until Sixtus V (1585-90) that work toward the grand vision would begin. An ambitious builder and a ruthless fighter against the Protestant revolution, Sixtus V "wished to 'quench the detestable memories of idolatry' and 'extirpate the idols exalted by pagans, such as pyramids, obelisks, and columns'" by moving Caligula's obelisk to the center of the square and "raise above it a Christian symbol 'to enhance the spirit of the Counter-Reformation' and 'exalt the mysteries of the Catholic religion.'" (21)

It was decided to move and raise the obelisk "as a symbol of the conquest of Church over paganism and Protestantism" (22) by enlisting the engineering talents of Domenico Fontana, who was told to "Eradicate the memory of the superstitions of antiquity by raising the greatest footing ever for the Holy Cross." (23)

The Pope hoped to have the obelisk raised in the Square on September 14, 1586, the Feast of the Exaltation of the Cross. With the efforts of 140 beasts and 800 men, masterful engineering, and an entire summer of work, the obelisk was removed, hauled, and stood upright by the 14th.

At its base were four gilt lions, meant to signify "how the ferocity and arrogance of the Gentiles had been suppressed by true religion, as the lions were by the obelisk." (24)

A formal ceremony of inauguration was held on September 26, including "the ritual purification and exorcising of the obelisk, and its subsequent consecration as a Christian monument . . . ." (25)

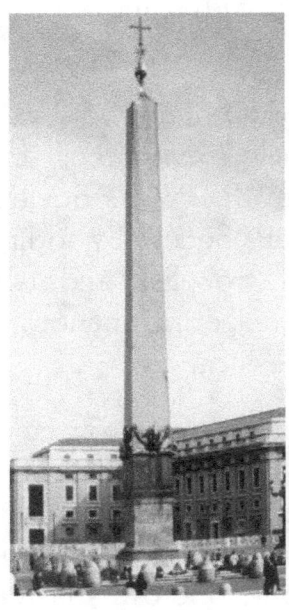

Photo Credit:
Michael Bausch

After a Mass, the cross that was to be placed upon the top of the obelisk was kissed, splashed with holy water, and blessed with the words, "See the Cross of the Lord! Flee adversaries, the Lion of Judah has conquered." (26)

After prayers and the singing of psalms, hyssop was used to sprinkle water to purify the sides of the monument. Then the bishop cut the sign of the cross on all sides in preparation for stationing the gilt cross atop the obelisk.

With this ceremony, Sixtus V accomplished his grand purpose, not to honor Egypt or glorify Rome, but to erect "the last tacit witness to the persecutions and sufferings of the Apostles and the early Christians in their heroic struggle for their faith against the evil forces of paganism." (27)

The stone, which witnessed the humiliation and suffering of the church, stood now as testimony to the joyful victory of the church. The Latin inscription at the top of the obelisk reads, "Sixtus V consecrated to the most holy Cross this stone torn away and stolen from its original place under Augustus and Tiberius Caesar." (28)

Lest we think all in Rome agreed with the money, effort, and ceremony dedicated to this project, there were those who thought it just like a Pope to join the Pharaohs and Caesars of old and raise an obelisk and put his name on it. Some also developed derogatory phrases with some obscene language. (29)

Nevertheless, the obelisk continued to figure both as a memorial to the fallen Christians in the ancient circus, and as an important architectural fixture in St. Peter's Square. Later, when Bernini redesigned St. Peter's Square by adding the elliptical colonnade (1657 ff.), the obelisk and two equidistant fountains would serve to stabilize and anchor the magnificent baroque approach to the basilica.

At that time, one approached St. Peter's via narrow lanes surrounded by houses and monasteries, to be surprised and awestruck by the sudden revealing of the square. Even now, with all of those houses and streets cleared in favor of the wide and straight Via della Conciliazione, one can still feel the power of the obelisk-anchored square.

To summarize, the obelisk represented an important symbolism to Egyptian, Roman, and Papal authorities. Crafting, transporting, erecting, lowering, and re-erecting these colossal pillars required the dedication of enormous human and financial resources.

The obelisk contained religious and political symbolism, whether it stood sentry at the entrance of an Egyptian temple, proclaimed the divinity of a Roman emperor from the spina of his circus, or extolled the victory of the Pope over protestant heretics.

There was also a humble and reverential tradition associated with the obelisk at St. Peter's Square, as ordinary Christians came to understand the stone to be a mute witness to the martyrdom of Peter and others during Nero's reign in the first century.

This magnificent stone serves as an architectural anchor for the baroque piazza that draws pilgrims towards the Basilica of St. Peter. The obelisk continues to represent purpose and significance to us, as the stone has for thousands of years of humanity in Heliopolis, Alexandria, and Rome.

Part 2: The Obelisk and Sacred Space

One of my personal interests in studying the St. Peter's Square obelisk was not only to learn its story but to try to understand my own reflective experience with the obelisk as "spiritually invigorating and emotionally powerful encounters with the Divine which emerge in part from imaginative identification with the historical events commemorated in the sacred space." (30)

That's a pretty dense way of saying that when we stop to pay attention to sacred spaces, we might find they are more than their time and history and might connect to our own spiritual awareness.

Urban Holmes' definition of what constitutes "spirituality" serves as an operating definition for me:

" . . . a human capacity for relationship with that which transcends sense phenomena; this relationship is perceived by the subject as an expanded or heightened consciousness independent of the subject's efforts, given substance in the historical setting, and exhibits itself in creative action in the world." (31)

A second definition, offered by Ellen Ross, speaks to me of the nature of the power of sacred space as:

" . . . specific geographical locations that have gained recognition on account of their association with particular historical events . . . (and which) function to connect believers to the Divine." (32)

Taken together, these definitions offer glimpses into the personal spiritual stimulation that the sacred space of St. Peter's Square offers. Both Holmes and Ross suggest the historical is an important ingredient in spiritual experience, first as a basic aspect of a spiritual relationship and second as a process, namely an "imaginative identification with historical events."

For me, seeing the obelisk and the surrounding grandeur of St. Peter's was first an architectural experience. I felt the sense of what Bernini sought to accomplish, to have the viewer feel the strength and magnificence of the Church Triumphant and then to be drawn toward the basilica itself. The architect has accomplished his aim: to draw every viewer closer to the worship space.

Even as the square has a Renaissance stability and order to it, there is also a Baroque energy that sucks the viewer in, drawing us closer to the worship center.

"Drawn into the basilica by the elliptical colonnade, the 'arms of the church,' we are aware that each step along the way is 'almost a succession of tableaux' and that we are a part of a grand design whose purpose is 'eloquent praise of the Church Triumphant.'" (33)

This is accomplished by a relatively narrow entrance, the widening of the colonnade, and then a narrowing again as one approaches the facade of St. Peter's. Human energy represented in groups of people moving toward and from the basilica also draws the viewer/participant toward the worship center.

Once inside, the participant is drawn ever closer toward the front of the sanctuary and the Cathedra Petri. As one leaves the basilica, the obelisk stands as a reminder of the Church Victorious.

After the initial experience suggested and created by the architecture of St. Peter's Square, I was also taken with what Ross calls the "imaginative identification with historical events." It would take two visits and reading in between those visits to be able to summon an imaginative vision of what happened on the site that made it the place of such architecture.

Without knowledge of the historical connection of obelisk to basilica, the site for me would be less one of historical significance and more of architectural significance.

But by reading and viewing diagrams of the original use of the site, namely as an imperial circus, used at one time to punish and kill Christians for Roman entertainment, I was able to imaginatively capture a spiritual identification with those martyrs.

As I stood near the obelisk, I could visualize the elliptical layout of the circus, could see the obelisk looming over the racetrack, could imagine the human torches lighting the night sky, could hear the crowds, and could see the crucifixions on the spina. It was a terrible image and one I did not wish to linger with, but in that moment I could simultaneously feel the peaceful sense brought by the piazza and basilica as they stood in memory of the fallen.

The spirit of the place is suggested in a different time and place by Abraham Lincoln's dedication of the Gettysburg National Cemetery: " . . . we cannot dedicate, we cannot consecrate, we cannot hallow, this ground. The brave men, living and dead, who struggled here, have consecrated it, far above our poor power to add or to detract." (34)

To know that the obelisk stood near where these Christians were murdered transports me from then to now and back again. It is history. It was real. Peter left the peaceful life of the Galilee and preached the good news of Jesus Christ to the congregations in Rome. They suffered together. He who once abandoned Jesus now took up his own cross in testimony to the power of the Resurrection.

Ellen Ross observes how a place can provide "encounters with the Divine" (35):

– sacred space is important to biblical faith because events happened in actual places and with living persons

– specific geographical places "associated with salvation

history are perceived as potent mediators of divine presence."

– early Christian women visited biblical sites to "celebrate, rejuvenate, and nourish their own faiths."

– pilgrimage to biblical sites helped these same women "re-experience such events through imagination and visualization."

– such visits encouraged a sense of belonging to a community of tradition, and through that experience "to the healing and sustaining power of God in the world."

– by reliving events that took place on a site, persons are able to grasp "the spiritual significance of the past" as it is "transported" to the present

– pilgrims experience the meaning of scripture and the earliest traditions of the church by "locating themselves in the historical, physical, concrete world where its narratives happened."

Her observations summarize what happened for me at St. Peter's and conveniently put into words that which was in my heart. In addition to "re-experienc(ing the) events through imagination and visualization" my experience served to "rejuvenate and nourish" my faith.

As one who prefers the concrete to the abstract, it has been important to my faith to be present at sites where biblical stories have happened.

As one who has gravitated toward the life and teachings of Jesus, my travel experiences to Galilee, Qumran, and Jerusalem have stimulated new awareness about the biblical record.

Not having placed much learning emphasis upon the individual apostles, coming to St. Peter's changed all that for me. I became aware that my faith was becoming nourished by this physical proximity to the final resting place of Peter.

I'd been to his house in Capernaum and seen the beauty of Galilee. His closeness to Jesus, his missionary zeal as evidenced by his life in Rome, and his martyrdom with other Christians all testify to the power of Christ's Resurrection in his life. To stand there and visualize all of this served to rekindle my own faith and commitment as one called to service in the name of that same Christ.

Not content to stop here, as well I could, Ross' insights led me into other readings about the nature, design, and structure of sacred space. One concept that was introduced was the "geographies of religion," referring to the fact that while most world religions are discussed and experienced in temporal ways, such as worship in a particular time and reflections on past, present, and future time, there is a spatial dimension to religious life as well.

The spatial dimension incorporates both the literal aspects of a specific earthly place and the symbolic or interpretive aspects of that space. My work on the obelisk at St. Peter's uses that method of seeking to understand how that obelisk came to that particular place and how we might understand the symbolism of the obelisk at that place.

In his article "The Centre of Space: Construction and Discovery," philosopher and linguist Frits Staal suggests that humans, birds, and animals seek to center their space. Nest-building and home-building center and structure the lives of living things. Humans across cultures have erected ritual poles to represent both a central axis to their relationship to the world of heaven and earth and to fertility rituals.

People, just like birds and other animals and in a similar spirit, construct and discover centers of space. These are therefore not only reflections of particular myths or cultures but also express general structures that are characteristic of our innate nature. (36)

Viewing the obelisk in this context, we see its centering function in Egyptian, Roman, and Christian architecture, calling attention to the leadership that cause the obelisk to be placed in its position adjacent to religious sites, be they Egyptian temple, Roman circus, or Christian basilica.

History professor J. Donald Hughes records human efforts to honor the "Spirit of Place in the Western World" and suggests that while Catholic and Protestant pilgrimages have come to honor the spirit of place reflected in their churches and shrines, the modern Western mentality "denies that place has any spirit . . . (as)both capitalism and Marxism define land and what it contains as economic resources subject to use and regard spirit as fantasy." (37)

Our challenge is to "find the places where we connect with the larger cosmos, to keep them free of the impedimenta that would block access to the spirit, and to open ourselves to the values that come from those places." (38)

Certainly with the souvenir stands adjacent to St. Peter's and the distraction of whatever ecclesiastical and social positions the Vatican has recently declared, it is possible to lose sight of the ancient history and spirit of the place.

Awareness of the history of this site – and any site – offers the rich opportunity to recover and discuss the values that constitute the spirit of the place.

John Irwin, a senior fellow of advanced studies at the National Gallery of Art, has studied and written about monumental art for decades. In his many articles about cosmic pillars, columns, obelisks, and other forms of the "image of the world's axis" he suggests that "the building of sacred monuments had been first and foremost a 'rite,' whereby Man sought to identify himself with the source of Cosmic Order." (39)

In the case of our obelisk, we have seen how the Egyptians and Romans used the obelisk as a symbol of the power of the sun and the authority of the earthly ruler. By placing a cross over this symbol, the Church proclaimed a new interpretation, that Christ is the one who orders the Cosmos.

A more structured response to the idea of a "multivalent" obelisk is provided in the work of Daniel Stokols, a professor of social ecology. In his "People-Environmental Relations: Instrumental and Spiritual Views," he suggests three human orientations to physical environments.

The "minimalist" view "assumes that physical environments exert minimal or negligible influence on behavior, health, and well-being of their users." (40) This view would be typified by the "so what?" of the obelisk or by denying hat it has any power or influence in St. Peter's Square.

A second approach is the "instrumental view" that "views the physical environment as a means for achieving important behavioural and economic goals." (41)

We have seen how the Egyptians, the Romans, and the papacy have erected the obelisk as a way to influence the behavior of their constituencies and to proclaim a message of invincibility and strength to the public.

A third orientation is the "spiritual view" that understands environments to have an end in themselves rather than to be seen as either unimportant or serving a particular view. This view understands particular places as the area "to which people are drawn by virtue of their symbolic and affective qualities." (42)

The architecture of place is "becoming increasingly interested in history, culture, myth, and meaning." This report has followed this approach to the architectural use of the obelisk.

My own study has tried to uncover the layers of meanings and interpretations to which the St. Peter's obelisk points. Uncovering such interpretations and meanings is the work of the imagination, which in itself engages the human spirit in life-affirming activity.

One particular direction in this work that Stokols suggests is a system of "global icons" that "remind us of our common global interests and responsibilities." (43) The obelisk may well be a candidate for such a nomination, particularly as we note the changes of the meaning of the obelisk from Egyptian to Roman times, from the early Christian to the medieval papal times, and on to our current era.

To summarize, visits to St. Peter's Square, when equipped with a historical understanding of the site, a sense of the architectural purpose of the building and ornamentation, an involvement in a community of faith, and a vivid imagination, will offer a spiritual experience that transports one back in time.

Formal reflection and discussion will help provide the "so what?" of the experience and engage us in the work of personal and communal spiritual formation.

My own spiritual experience of the site, as stimulated by the symbolism of the obelisk, comes in deciding which symbolism I shall select as meaningful and true.

As I transport myself into the scenes of the martyrdom, experienced adjacent to the obelisk, I realize the true testimony to the work, mission, and ministry of Jesus of Nazareth, the crucified and risen Lord. I reject the symbolism of the Pharaoh, Caesar, and the Pope that uses the obelisk as a religious-political sign of their attempts at social control through a top-down stratified system where the privileged few lord over the masses of people.

Part 3: The Obelisk and Its Meanings

I have already mentioned how my personal understanding of the impact of St. Peter's Square is thickened by becoming aware of both the architecture and the early history of the site. What surprised me in my research was the amount of thought and degree of importance given the obelisk as a symbol.

What disturbed me was to realize that the obelisk, which has become an important historical marker for me, also was used by the papacy to try to centralize religious authority and theological interpretation, with the intent of both building an imperial papal state and silencing individuals or movements disagreeing with those same papal actions and interpretations.

What surprises and disturbs us about any symbol allows us to engage the various interpretations of its meaning.

Theologian James Poling, in his book on practical theology, suggests "Part of theology is interpretation. Interpretation involves disturbing the surface of consciousness through the use of symbols that are multivalent and therefore point beyond present consciousness to a new consciousness."(44)

What is the new consciousness generated by this "multivalent" (meaning having many values) symbol, this obelisk at St. Peter's Square?

First, it is a story of redemption.

The obelisk represented to ancient Egypt the imperial power of the Pharaoh and symbolized the hierarchical stratification of a society in which the elites claimed divine power and the underclasses were locked in the status of servitude.

The same obelisk was brought to Rome to symbolize its imperial power and stood as a decoration on the spine of the circus at the Vatican as a sundial and a visible reminder of the Caesar's imperial authority. The obelisk stood as silent witness to the torture and deaths of early Christians after the fire of Rome in 64 C.E.

The church moved the obelisk to its present position and aligned it with the dove on the inside of the sanctuary, placed a cross on its top, and exorcised its imperial power. The obelisk serves as a symbol of redemption, that in the suffering of the cross the kingdoms of the world lose their power.

Secondly, it is a memorial to the Christian martyrs.

The circus had come and gone, but the church carried the slain comrades in its memory. The obelisk stands both as a reminder of the crumbling of the empire and the ongoing life of the church. By venerating the named and unnamed saints, we carry forward the very tradition they died for. It is a reminder to carry on bravely in the mission the Gospels proclaim.

Thirdly, the obelisk may remind us of other people who are blamed for things that go wrong in society.

Just as Nero probably had the fires of Rome set and then blamed the Christians, so do we do the same. The bombing in Oklahoma City (1995) resulted in immediate blame of the Muslim community. Recent attempts to curb immigration into this country or to blame welfare recipients for our budget deficits are other examples of scapegoating societal problems onto certain groups of people.

Fourth, the obelisk as symbol reminds us of the larger task of theological education in the church.

Rebecca S. Chopp of Candler School of Theology discusses how theological education forms persons to be "symbolic constructors." Thinking about theological education as a participation in the symbolic will include the construction and engagement in present and future symbolic patterns as well as understanding and interpreting symbolic thought in past centuries.

She writes, "Students are taught the symbolic patterns of past centuries and should be taught how these symbols and ideas functioned within the practices of the time. But students and teachers also need to engage in the symbolic struggles of our day. Education . . . is about forming persons to be symbolic constructors, about training persons to be poets as well as interpreters."(45)

Part of this task is to engage people with symbols they find in daily life.

While leaving a burial service at a local cemetery with the funeral director, I showed him a few of the monuments that were obelisks. We noticed these were all in the older part of the cemetery.

He asked me what the obelisk was, and I gave him a thumbnail sketch of the Egyptian history and how obelisks from Egypt were moved to various locations in the world, including Rome, where they were used by the church to decorate the entrances to holy places. People have used that shape for millennia.

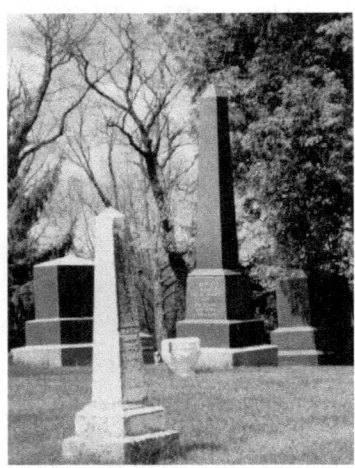

Photo Credit: Michael Bausch

We then started talking about how people generally don't take time to consider the symbolism of the past and don't question what a shape might mean or what it signified or signifies today.

This was an opportunity to do what professor Chopp suggests, which is to train people to be interpreters by becoming aware of the rich symbols that surround us in our daily living.

The next day, while sitting in a meeting at a Wisconsin church and looking out the window, the steeple of a Lutheran church across the street came into focus. On top of the steeple was an orb, upon which sat a cross. Here was the old Roman decoration of the St. Peter's obelisk – on a Lutheran church!

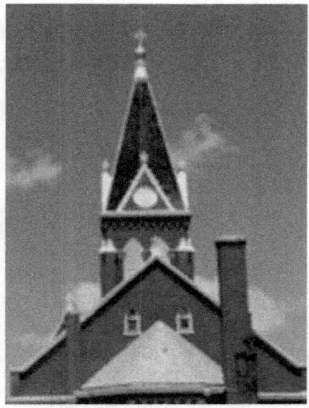

Photo credit: Michael Bausch

A few hours later I noticed another steeple, that of the local Roman Catholic church (below), and, sure enough, there were what appeared to be an orb and a cross.

I could understand it on the Catholic church, but the great irony of it being on the Lutheran Church made me want to ask the Lutherans if they knew why their steeple was designed in such a way and what it meant to them.

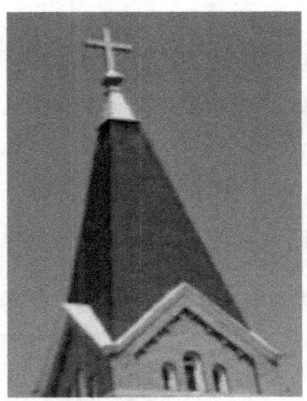

Photo credit: Michael Bausch

Then I noticed the steeple of the local United Methodist church, and instead of a cross there was a small obelisk on top of the steeple!

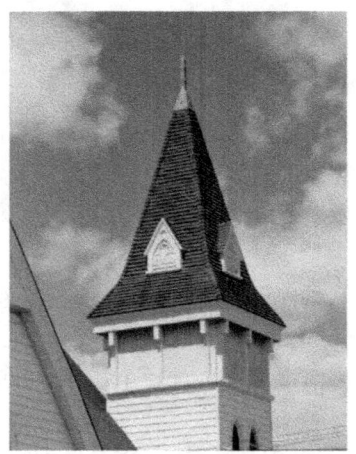

Photo credit: Michael Bausch

If we understand steeples to function like obelisks, pointing skyward, we become aware of the way human buildings seek to pierce heaven, that there is a relationship between earthly and heavenly realms.

How does this help us become "poets as well as interpreters" and how does this contribute to the "symbolic struggles of our day?" As we have seen, the obelisk has historically represented imperial power.

When Sixtus V had it moved to its present location, he had planned on a large statue of Jesus holding a golden cross. This plan died with this Pope of only five years.

The simple, tiny cross that adorns this obelisk, as well as most every other obelisk in Rome, offers a poignant counterpoint to the domination of the stone obelisk. Where imperialism and tyranny reign, the cross remains as a reminder of the community of faith.

To mix Christian metaphors, just as yeast is small and unseen and yet a powerful influence upon the ultimate shape of the bread and just as the tiny mustard seeds grow into wildflowers that can ultimately take over a farmer's field, so does that small cross make its power known as ultimate victor. Obelisk, i.e., imperial power, is ever subservient to the community formed by the Cross.

In James Russell Lowell's hymn, "Once to Every Man and Nation," written during the Mexican-American War in 1845, a war he opposed, the second verse echoes the experience of the Christian martyrs at the obelisk in the seventh decade of the first century C.E.:

"By the light of burning martyrs, Jesus' bleeding feet I track, Toiling up new Calvaries ever With the cross that turns not back; New occasions teach new duties, Time makes ancient good uncouth; They must upward still and onward, Who would keep abreast of truth." (46)

For the martyrs of Rome, burned or crucified less than 40 years after Jesus' death, the spina of the Vatican circus became their Calvary. The obelisk stood in mute testimony to the power of imperial gods who proclaimed a world view of domination over those who would not relinquish their freedoms, their homeland, and their faith.

When the cross was placed upon that same obelisk, there was a reversal of the energy flow and a proclamation of a new view of life (Lowell, v. 3): "Though the cause of evil prosper, Yet 'tis truth alone is strong, Truth forever on the scaffold, Wrong forever on the throne. Yet that scaffold sways the future, And, behind the dim unknown, Standeth God within the shadow Keeping watch above his own." (47)

Closing: A Holy Obelisk

After early Hebrews crossed the Jordan River and first entered The Promised Land, Joshua instructed that the people raise a pillar of stones so in the days to come, when children asked why those stones were there, people could tell the story of God's mighty deeds as the community moved forward into a new way of living.

"Those twelve stones, which they had taken out of the Jordan, Joshua set up in Gilgal, saying to the Israelites, 'When your children ask their parents in time to come, "What do these stones mean?" then you shall let your children know (the story) . . . ' so that all the peoples of the earth may know that the hand of the Lord is mighty, and so that you may fear the Lord your God forever." (Joshua 4:20-24)

I asked the same question of the obelisk in St. Peter's Square, "Why is this stone here?"

After reading and personal reflection, I am able to answer how that stone came to be in that place and what it meant to the various peoples who fashioned it, transported it, and looked at it.

As I visualize the martyrdom it witnessed, I gain a reverential sense of the site and its sacredness. As I travel to that holy site with other pilgrims, I am able to communicate the poignancy of the place and the triumph it represents. It was here where witnesses to the Risen Christ became martyrs. Their witness strengthens my faith and firms its foundation.

The granite stone of the obelisk points Christians to the "living stone" of the Christ and to a call to be joined with him in his work: "Come to him, a living stone, though rejected by mortals yet chosen and precious in God's sight, and like living stones, let yourselves be built into a spiritual house . . . ." (I Peter 2:4-5)

About This Chapter

This chapter was originally a paper prepared as a "project in spirituality" in partial fulfillment of requirements for the Doctor of Ministry program of the Minnesota Consortium of Theological Schools. By reflecting upon my personal experiences at St. Peter's Square in Rome and by researching the history and symbolism of the Egyptian obelisk in St. Peter's Square, I was to show it possible to identify the ways this sacred space affected my personal spirituality. The original title was, "The Personal Spiritual Significance of the Site and Symbolism of the Obelisk at St. Peter's Square, Rome" and was submitted on May 22, 1995.

The end notes and bibliography may be found on pages 107-112.

Chapter 8

SICILY: SHORT POEMS

Poems Inspired by Observations During My First Trip to Italy 1993

26 Drinks

High on his balcony a man hangs his undershirts out to dry

While a woman leans over her railing and spits.

On the street below someone retrieves a saw from a car as

Two girls walk hand in hand, black hair blowing in the wind.

A couple strolls with their children, and a

Tow truck lifts a car from the street only to put it back.

Four cars park behind four other cars.

The bank clock flashes the time, date and temperature as

Girls on motorbikes beep on the street.

Friends link arms, as lights flash upon the department store

trance.

Some walkers avoid him

Others pass by him without care.

I watch from the sixth floor

And he stands alone, 26 drinks into his wine.

Rendezvous

With her passport secure behind the hotel desk, she

Walks towards the sea.

Shoes clack the pavement and her dress sways blithely

With her hips.

She looks to either side of the narrow street, noticing

Families stopping for dinner.

She sits at the table nearest the doorway and sips

Iced tea as she waits.

Her Graeco-Italian god quickly enters the bar

Thick-maned and half her age.

He orders a scotch and gets her another tea

Paying for both when they leave.

Later, after they make love, she calmly glances at the wall

Fulfilled by her journey.

A Day in the Life: Sicilian Birds

Agrigento Lido:

A rooster declares the morning

Proclaiming nature's sway over the waking village.

Segesta:

Songbirds nest in the high reaches of the abandoned temple

Trilling their blessing over the sacred site.

Erice:

The white dove bobs over the smoothed cobblestones

Declaring peace in the narrow streets.

Men

When the bars close

There is one place to go

The corner stand by the park

They serve you your beer

And good things to eat

A place to talk in the dark.

One night the men

Had gathered around

In that Sicilian place.

She came to order

A sight so rare

The air suspended in grace.

(Inspired by the story of Archimedes, in Ortygia, Syracusa.)

Naked

Teacher told the story of Archimedes

How he sat in his bathtub and watched the water rise.

He noticed his body displaced its own weight in water

And from then on honest measurements were possible.

She told how he leapt out of the tub and ran down the street

Naked.

As he cried "Eureka!" "Eureka!" the class laughed.

Late one night I walked the street

Behind the gelateria in the park

And found Archimedes' lane

Cobbled with large blocks of cut stone

Looking the same as when he ran upon it

Naked.

Mental image becomes feet upon the street:

Archimedes ran these stones

Announcing to the world His excited discovery.

Classroom laughter fades

Through all these years of displacement.

Truth lived between the real and the imagined

Naked.

Archimedes' Distraction

Everyday problems occupied his thought.

Ortygia demanded solutions.

He sat in his tub and found the way to

True mercantile measurements.

He jumped up and ran down the street with

Nary a towel to proclaim he had found it!

He set up his mirrors and learned they burned

So he took them to the point overlooking the

Sea and waited for the ships to come.

The People rejoiced he could burn the fleet!

Alone in his study he pondered the perfect

Mathematical equations of life.

The soldier demanded he go to the chief

But Archimedes had better on his mind.

Distracted he wondered if he had found

The secret that all had sought

Impatient the soldier stuck in his sword

And we shall never know.

Chapter 9

BERKELEY: ABU GHRAIB

When the Colombian artist Fernando Botero was looking for a place to exhibit his work "Abu Ghraib," only the University of California-Berkeley would accept his art. Other schools found it too controversial.

At the time, in January 2007, I was minister-in-residence at the Pacific School of Religion in Berkeley, California, and I had the chance to hear Botero speak about his work. What follows is my write-up of the occasion:

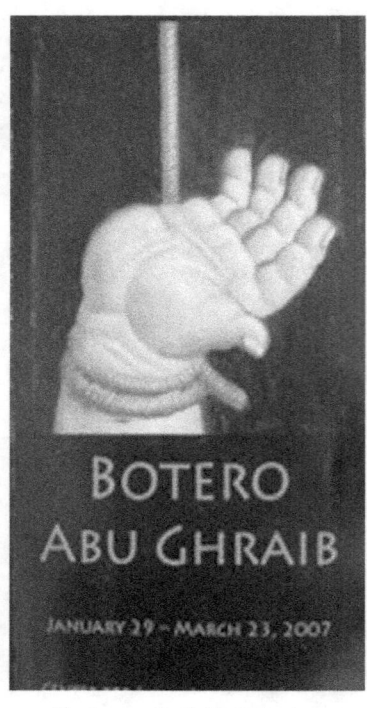

Photo credit: Exhibit Poster

It has been three years since the world saw digital photographs of U.S. soldiers torturing and taunting detainees at Abu Ghraib, the Iraqi prison. Now for the first time, an internationally known artist has sketched and painted scenes of this suffering based on photographs and written reports of what went on inside the prison.

Fernando Botero, 74, a Columbian-born painter and sculptor now living in Paris, began working on his sketches as response to the anger and outrage he felt as he first read newspaper reports of the torture while on an overseas flight.

In 14 months, he produced 47 oil paintings, now on display to March 25 at the Doe Library on the University of California-Berkeley campus, in an exhibit jointly sponsored by the Center for Latin American Studies, Boalt Hall Law School, and the Doe Library. The exhibit is the only public showing in the United States to date.

On January 29, Botero was introduced to a standing-room-only audience of more than 400 people at the International House on the Berkeley campus by Harley Shaiken, chair of the Center for Latin American Studies, who said, "Art is a permanent accusation . . . that at moments of crisis has an exceptional role."

Botero was joined on stage by Robert Haas, U.S. poet laureate in 1995-97, who had been asked to lead the public conversation with Botero. Responding to a question about why he produced these paintings, Botero spoke about his "rage and anger" as he developed his early sketches provoked by what he had seen and read, seeking to "give it testimony and not remain silent." While his sketches were drawn in anger, he said he painted "with love" because "for me it was important to give back dignity to these people."

Haas noted that the paintings have "a religious quality" to them, not only through their stimulation of the "moral imagination about the victims" but in the "echoes of the stations of the cross and the martyrologies." "These figures were almost biblical," he said, "an 'ecce homo' of what man is capable of." Botero responded by saying that as he painted, "all of this," including Christ and his suffering, "was in the back of my mind."

Botero's career began as a young man of 19 when, after a brief period in Paris, he went to Florence and painted copies of the works of the religious subjects of great masters like Giotto, Masaccio, and others. He was particularly moved by Giotto's "voluminous figures," and, indeed, his Abu Ghraib figures share a similar volume in relationship to the small space of the cells in which they are kneeling, hanging, or lying. In one agonized scene a small glowing window can be seen in the background – "Was it a small symbol of hope?" "Exactly," Botero replied. "I wanted to contrast the atmosphere of terror with hope."

When asked why he chose to paint pictures of these scenes of U.S.-inflicted torture rather than show the results of terrorist violence, Botero responded by saying he has always had a sympathy with the United States and appreciated the "ideal of compassion conveyed by America," but that "this torture was unexpected . . . this was why . . . ."

Haas spoke of an Egyptian journalist, who, when hearing that the United States had tortured detainees, said, "A light has been turned off in the world." Haas then told the audience, "Maybe these paintings will help turn the light back on."

Chapter 10

AVATAR (2009)

Yes, it's been a few years since this film came out, and I saw it with 3-D glasses in a Madison, Wisconsin, movie theater. Yet just this summer (2017), while reading two different books (listed at the end of this chapter), I found references to the ancient debate between Pelagius and Augustine, two Christian theologians who lived in the fifth century.

While most people haven't heard of either one of these men, this caught my attention because back in 2009 I'd found a connection with Pelagius, Augustine, and James Cameron's worldwide box-office sensation, *Avatar*.

What in the world were these fellows from fifth-century Egypt and Palestine doing in a 21st-century Hollywood movie?

To find out more of the biblical – and theological – connections I'd found in *Avatar*, read on!

There's plenty not to like about James Cameron's sensational film. On the eve of the film's release in Italy, the Vatican called it "simplistic" and full of "pseudo-doctrines . . . that turn ecology into the religion of the millennium."

A *New York Times* reviewer said the same thing a few weeks earlier, calling the film a "long apologia for pantheism . . . ."

A couple of young men with whom I'd chatted said the film was great for the technical effects but not so good as a story, since that has been told and retold many times already. "This film," one said, "will be remembered for the technology."

An *Onion* film review called it "supremely goofy."

Yet people continue to see it, and the film is the highest grossing film, raking in $2.8 billion since its release from viewers not only in the United States but around the world.

I loved it. There were several points where I responded with deep feelings: in the exquisitely beautiful scenes of the graceful, floating tree seeds, for example, and in the horror of metal gunships spewing destructive power upon a pristine Eden-like land. There is little escaping the emotional and physical power of 3-D visual effects joined with full surround sound.

At one point I ducked as an object seemed to be flying right at me! At times I wondered how bugs got into the theater on a cold winter's day, when in reality (virtual reality, that is) they were actually in the movie.

Avatar is a work of art. Unlike many films (I think of the popular *The Hangover* from around the same time (2009), there is a whole curriculum waiting to be drawn out of this film. With so many people seeing it and so many commenting on it, the film is a ready-made study piece. It can be an exciting way to enliven 1) youth and adult education 2) a sermon series and 3) efforts to practice talking together about the media we experience.

As the film's musical theme "I See You" declares, when we look at another living being or at life itself, when we truly look to see, we enter into a sacred relationship. There is much that this film invites. As theologian Paul Tillich reminded the church, intentional theological reflection begins with a relationship with life that then stimulates questions.

At its best, when the church engages the questions honored and provoked by art, it serves as a bridge between culture and biblical theology.

We encourage a depth of inquiry by raising questions; we encourage dialogue by encouraging the drawing of comparisons and contrasts between a work of art and the biblical witness; we notice a prophetic socio-political critique and perceive an incarnational embrace of story as parable; we model a way of living, thinking, and being that honors the world, the arts, culture, and history while being faithful to the meta-narrative of biblical tradition.

The next part of my reflections will focus on the mythical/biblical references I find in the film. While most critics have uncovered the obvious mythical references, most of these same critics are illiterate when it comes to biblical material. They miss the irony of a line from the film when the corporate executive ordering the destruction of the Home Tree and its sacred seeds blurts, "It's just a sacred fern, for Christ's sake!"

James Cameron is more aware than we think when it comes to biblical theology. Those who only see a "theology of pantheism" have completely missed Cameron's deep – and amusing – theology of grace, with full reference to the ancient/modern Augustinian-Pelagian debate.

Cameron's *Avatar* (2009) and Dali's *The Burning Giraffe* (1937)

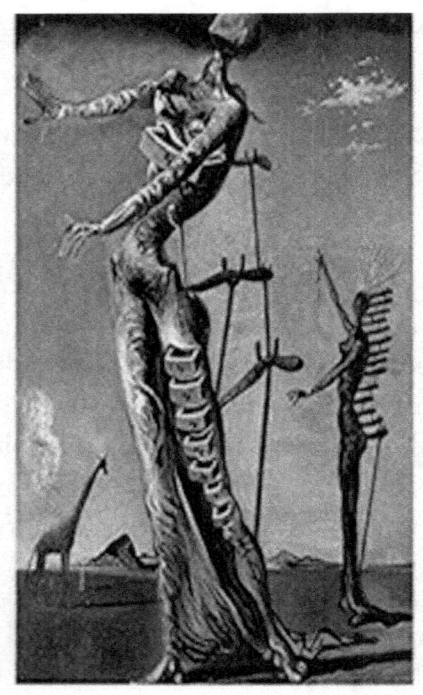

Source:
Wikipedia.org/wiki/The_Burning_Giraffe

A few hours after watching *Avatar* I went to a favorite Costa Rican Cafe for supper. I was seated at a small table near the door that faced a wall. As I waited to order, I noticed directly in front of me a Salvador Dali print with two elongated figures in the foreground and, off in the background, a smaller figure. As I looked at the smaller figure I realized that it was an animal on fire. This strange and striking image took me back to *Avatar*, in which there is a short scene of a running horse on fire. The picture was one of pure horror resulting from the cruelties inflicted upon the living beings in the film's Pandora. Was James Cameron making a reference to Salvador Dali?

In the foreground of the Dali print are two long, blue women. The women of Pandora in *Avatar* are long and blue. Dali called his women in the print before me "tailbone women," and the Pandora creatures did have tails! Coincidence? The collective unconscious at work in the artistic imagination?

Dali used the image of the burning giraffe in his 1930

film, *L'Age d'Or* (The Golden Age) and again in his 1937 *The Invention of Monsters*. He apparently saw this as a premonition of World War II, and his burning giraffe is an image of "the masculine cosmic apocalyptic monster."

The "monsters" of war in *Avatar* are steel helicopters, the large mother ship-plane and the massive robotic "soldiers" piloted by individuals inside these walking structures.

Cameron's Colonel Quaritch embodies this "masculine cosmic apocalyptic monster" in the film. This makes him, too, an "avatar" of sorts.

I've been unable as of yet to locate any confirmation by Cameron of this reference to Dali's work. It may be I am stretching this a bit much, but the parallels are very striking.

The juxtaposition of the Dali image with the scene of the burning horse in the film would be an excellent starting point for a discussion or sermon about some of the issues raised in the film. An additional image suggestion would be Picasso's "Guernica" from the same time period and the terrified horse in the center of the painting.

Biblical Narratives in *Avatar* (2009)

When one of the main characters of a film is named "Dr. Grace Augustine," one's theological ears need to perk up! Augustine of Hippo was called "the Doctor of Grace." He and a fellow named Pelagius argued over the doctrine of original sin and the meaning of grace. I suggest that James Cameron was not promoting pantheism in this film but settling in his own way the ancient arguments about grace and awarding Pelagius (judged a heretic by the church) the winner's prize.

Sin and Grace

One discussion thread for *Avatar* is indeed this: The concept of sin and grace as found in the Garden of Eden in the biblical narrative, compared and contrasted with that found in the garden planet of Pandora. While investigating the ancient debate between Augustine and Pelagius, this study thread would also include evaluating questions raised by various critics concerned about more modern concerns about pantheism, neo-paganism, etc. in the film.

Questions to include might be: What is pantheism? How is pantheism different from eco-spirituality? What is panentheism? What is Mother Goddess religion? What is paganism? Are these to be feared? Why or why not? Where might we find examples of this in the film's story and dialogue? How does this debate get played out in various church and non-church circles? What are the issues at stake e.g., political, social, cultural, economic, moral, and religious?

Another thread related to this is stimulated by the fact that this story takes place on a mythical planet named "Pandora." What is the Greek myth of Pandora about? Is Pandora an equivalent of the biblical Eve? Are the curses that emerge from Pandora's jar (or, as it is mistranslated, "box") similar to those God gives Adam and Eve?

Moving on, the people of Pandora are called "Na'vi," and the biblical Hebrew word for prophet is "nav'i," or "mouth of God." What does the filmmaker intend to tell us with this reference? How do these people in the movie live and function like biblical prophets, then and now?

The female Na'vi character, Neytiri, gives Jacob a pomegranate-like fruit from a tree. His eyes seem to open up at that point to really behold the beauty of where he is. How does this fruit scene compare and contrast with the fruit scene in the story in the Garden of Eden? How do the two sacred trees in Pandora compare to the two in Eden?

The Jacob and Esau Story

Besides parallels in the Genesis account of the Garden of Eden, there are comparisons in the film to the Jacob/Esau story also found in the Book of Genesis. While the comparisons might be weak and stretched too much, they yet invite some imaginative consideration.

In *Avatar*, Jacob has a twin brother named Tom. Jacob is translated from the Hebrew to mean "supplanter." In the film, it was Tom, Jacob's brother, who was to be the avatar. With his untimely and tragic death, Jacob takes his place, a kind of supplanting.

After seeing *Avatar*, it is interesting to read the story of Jacob's ladder in Genesis 28:10-17. There is a communication between one realm and another, heaven and earth, with many winged creatures (angels) flying around. A blessing is given that through Jacob all the families of the earth shall be blessed. There is divine assurance of ongoing presence and guidance, and then Jacob awakens, realizing he has been traveling between heaven and earth, the "house of God" and the "gate of heaven."

Later, in Genesis 32, Jacob wrestles with the mysterious angel, gains a limp, and has a name change. His new name is "Israel," or one who struggles or strives with God. As some suggest *Avatar* advocates reverting to some kind of nature-worshiping "tribal existence," clearly the parallel with the coming tribal confederacy and covenant community of ancient Israel in Jacob's story might fit – at least in an imaginative and inspired preaching context!

After all, the covenant of "shalom" extends peace to every aspect of creation including the land, the water, the sky, the animals, and people!

John 1:1-9, 14

A third connection to a biblical narrative might be found in the Gospel of John and the prologue of the first chapter with its theological concepts of light and word. Light and Word translate into life, as at the beginning in Genesis 1, and both light and word become flesh, a human being, one who embodies word, light, and love.

Might it make some sense to briefly and lightly touch on the imaginative correlation of the Hindu "avatar" in reference to this Christian "epiphany" to draw out comparisons and contrasts?

Other snippets of interesting material:

a. There are coffin-like structures shown throughout the film, with juxtaposed scenes from a real coffin holding Jake's brother to the avatar-pods. There is no getting around the themes these evoke: death, life, rebirth, renewal, and transformation.

b. Noting the worship practices depicted in the film: singing at the sacred tree, honoring ancestors, prayer, laying on of hands, and the presence of ritual at sacred place.

c. Treating relationships with nature and living things with respect, honoring a sacred relationship. While some may see this as pantheism, it seems more of an honoring of the sanctity of all things. Note the blessing/saying "grace" before taking the life of an animal and/or the connection with horses and birds as the Na'vi linked strands of hair with the strands and fibers of another's life.

d. The clash of different systems of belief: one in "military fact" and power and another in the sacredness of deity and/or nature. There is a clash of cultures: military, natural, and scientific.

e. The relationship of the term "avatar" in Hindu mythology/theology with "epiphany" in Greco-Roman mythology/political theology and in Christian theology.

f. How does the final scene parallel the final scene of Mel Gibson's film *The Passion of the Christ* (2004), and what are we to make of it?

g. Just as one world is shown to be of advanced technology, is another world is shown as one of advanced spirituality?

h. The Hallelujah Mountains figure beautifully in the film and are the closing images as the credits roll. "Hallelujah" means "praise God" in biblical Hebrew.

i. The connection with the themes found in Dali's *Burning Giraffe* as mentioned previously.

j. The valuable mineral the corporation seeks, with the aid of its mercenaries, is called "Unobtanium." The unobtainable has a high price.

k. Lines in the film that invite some discussion (Without a script in front of me, these lines are what I thought I heard while watching the film, and I wrote them down in the darkened theater while wearing 3-D glasses!):

"I was a warrior who dreamed he would bring peace."

"The Great Mother does not take sides. She protects the balance of life."

"The wealth of the world is all around us."

"Grace is hit."

"I'm a scientist; I don't believe in fairy tales."

Did Jake call out "holy snake!" as one of the snake-headed creatures flew out of the Mother Tree?

l. The theme song, "I See You," sings of the film's joyful embrace of conscientious, intentional, life-honoring relationships and the "colors of love." Where is love in the film? Is the full complexity of the term "love" there, in the biblical sense? Do we find in the film an implied shallow "pantheism," or is it more of what we find in John's Gospel and the phrase "For God so loved the world . . . "? Doesn't John affirm that the world is imbued with love? Isn't love embedded in each creature, all of life, the animate and inanimate?

All of this may seem a little too detailed, but there are great pleasure and learning that come out of these deeper reflections. One of my university students, after seeing and hearing my lecture (with film clips) on the biblical themes in *Spider-Man 2* (2004), asked, "Can't you just enjoy a movie without having to go so deep?" I said, "Yes, but it's not as much fun."

Author's note: The books I read in the summer of 2017, as mentioned at the beginning of this chapter, were Harvey Cox's *The Market As God* (2016), in which he dedicates an entire chapter to looking at how and why Augustine's theology came to be viewed as "better" than that of Pelagius, restoring Pelagius as one whose views should be reconsidered, and Thomas Cahill's *How The Irish Saved Civilization* (1995), in which he notes the debate and, as with most other conventional scholars, dismisses Pelagius as being too positive towards human nature. Cox, at least, shows it was big-money interests, rather than the merits of their arguments, that helped Augustine win the battle.

End Notes for Chapters 2, 3, 4, and 5

1. Tom Buckley, "The Discovery of Tutankhamun's Tomb" in *Treasures of Tutankhamun* (New York: The Metropolitan Museum of Art, 1976) 13.

2. Umberto Baldini, "Sculpture" in *The Complete Work of Michelangelo* by Mario Salmi et al. (New York: Reynal and Company, 1967) 104. Baldini reports suggestions that Hercules may have been a model for this *David*, and there is some thought that Michelangelo carved his *David* as a mirror image of his earlier, but lost, Hercules. I suggest the calm repose of the Hellenistic *Apollo Belvedere* to be similar to that of *David*.

3. Jane Dillenberger, *Secular Art With Sacred Themes* (Nashville: Abingdon Press, 1969) 1.

4. N. E. Thing Enterprises, *Magic Eye: A New Way of Looking at the World* (Kansas City: Andrews and McMeel, 1993) 4

5. Dillenberger, 1.

6. Mike Wilks, *The Ultimate Alphabet* (New York: Henry Holt and Company, 1986) 1. This is a book of twenty-six pictures, each illustrating one letter of the alphabet, containing as few as thirty items (letter "X") and as many at 1,229 items (letter "S"). Viewing this book is a "looking" identification process more than a "seeing" process as defined in this paper and is an enjoyable and challenging experience.

7. John and Jane Dillenberger, Paul Tillich, *On Art and Architecture* (New York: The Crossroad Publishing Company, 1987) 235.

8. Helen Fisher, *Anatomy of Love* (New York: Fawcett

Columbine, 1992) 23-29

9. Jane Dillenberger, *Image and Spirit in Sacred and Secular Art* (New York: Crossroad, 1990) 2

10. Ibid.

11. William Manchester, *A World Lit Only by Fire: The Medieval Mind and the Renaissance* (New York: Little, Brown and Company, 1992) 91

12. Erwin Panofsky, *Meaning in the Visual Arts* (Garden City: Doubleday Anchor Books, 1955)

13. Dillenberger, *Image and Spirit*, 12.

14. Wilson Yates, *The Arts in Theological Education* (Atlanta: Scholars Press, 1987) 135.

15. Umberto Baldini, 104.

16. Rick Steves and Gene Openshaw, *Mona Winks: Self-Guided Tours of Europe's Top Museums* (Santa Fe: John Muir Publishing, 1988) 308.

17. Umberto Baldini, 104.

18. John Dillenberger. *A Theology of Artistic Sensibilities: The Visual Arts and the Church* (New York: Crossroad, 1969) 78.

19. James Hall, *Dictionary of Subjects and Symbols in Art* (New York: Harper and Row, 1974) 148.

20. Ibid., 25.

2 I. Rick Steves and Gene Openshaw, 293.

22. Bernard Denvir, *Art Treasures of Italy* (New York: Galahad Books, 1980) 182.

23. James Russell Lowell, "Once to Every Man and Nation" in *Pilgrim Hymnal* (Boston: The Pilgrim Press, 1958) No. 441, verse 3.

24. Harvard University Students. *Let's Go Budget Guide to Italy 1994* (Cambridge: St. Martin's Press, 1994) 54.

25. John and Jane Dillenberger, Paul Tillich, *On Art and Architecture*, 106.

26. Ibid., 232.

27. Rick Steves and Gene Openshaw, 362.

28. Oreste Ferrari, *Masterpieces of the Vatican* (London: Thames and Hudson, Ltd. 1971) 77.

29. *Baedeker's Rome* (New York: Prentice Hall Press, no date) 152.

30. Jane Dillenberger, *Style and Content*, 174-175.

31. Ibid., 178.

32. Wylie Sypher, *Four Stages of Renaissance Style* (Garden City: Doubleday and Company, 1956) 188-189.

33. John Dillenberger, *A Theology of Artistic Sensibilities*, 242.

34. Ibid., 256.

35. Ibid., 242.

36. Mike Wilks, 3.

End Notes and Bibliography For Chapter 7

1. Erik Iversen, *Obelisks in Exile* (Copenhagen: Gad. 1968) 17

2. Ibid., 16

3. Bern Dibner, *Moving the Obelisks: A Chapter in Engineering History* (Cambridge: MIT Press, 1970) 12

4. E. A. Wallis Budge, *Cleopatra's Needles and Other Egyptian Obelisks* (London: Religous Tract Society, 1926) 255

5. Iversen, 19

6. John Humphrey, *Roman Circuses: Arenas For Chariot Racing* (Berkeley: University of California Press, 1985) 270

7. Ibid., 270

8. Ibid., 94

9. Dibner, 17-18

10. John Henry Parker, *The Archaeology of Rome. Vol. IV. Obelisks* (Oxford: J. Park and Co. 1874) 5

11. Humphrey, 175

12. Ibid., 175

13. Umberto M. Fasola, *Peter and Paul in Rome* (Rome: Vision, 1980) 107

14. Will Durant, *Caesar and Christ* (New York: Simon and Schuster, 1944)

15. Fasola, 107

16. Iversen, 22

17. Fasola, 105-106

18. Ibid., 117

19. Iversen, 23

20. Peter Tompkins, *The Magic of Obelisks* (New York: Harper and Row, 1981) 18

21. Ibid., 21

22. Ibid.

23. Ibid., 23

24. Iversen, 37

25. Ibid., 38

26. Ibid.

27. Ibid., 41

28. Ibid., 39

29. Tompkins, 37-39. Tompkins reports such thoughts and adds that some locals referred to the obelisk with crude references reflecting, among other things, it's ancient phallic symbolisms.

30. Ellen Ross, "Diversities of Divine Presence: Women's Geography in the Christian Tradition" in *Sacred Places and Profane Spaces: Essays in the Geographies of Judaism. Christianity, and Islam* (Ed. Jamie Scott. New York: Greenwood Press, 1991) 94

31. Urban Tigner Holmes, *Spirituality for Ministry* (New York:

Harper & Row, 1982) 12

32. Ross, 94

33. Oreste Ferrari, *Masterpieces of the Vatican* (London: Thames and Hudson, Ltd. 1971) 77

34. Garry Wills, *Lincoln At Gettysburg* (New York: Simon and Schuster, 1992) 263

35. Ross, 98-101

36. Frits Staal, "The Centre of Space: Construction and Discovery" in *Concepts of Space Ancient and Modern* by Kapila Vatsyayan (New Delhi: Indira Gandhi National Centre for the Arts, 1991) 98

37. J. Donald Hughes, "Spirit of Place in the Western World" in *The Power of Place: Sacred Ground in Natural and Human Environments* by James A. Swan (Bath, U.K.: Gateway Books, 1993) 23.

38. Ibid., 25

39. John Irwin, "Origins of Form and Structure in Monumental Art" in *Concepts of Space Ancient and Modern* by Kapila Vatsyayan (New Delhi: Indira Gandhi National Centre for the Arts, 1991) 146

40. Daniel Stokols, "People-Environment Relations: Instrumental and Spiritual Views" in *The Power of Place: Sacred Ground in Natural and Human Environments* by James A. Swan (Bath, U.K.: Gateway Books, 1993) 347.

41. Ibid., 349

42. Ibid., 350

43. Ibid., 357

44. James N. Poling and Donald E. Miller, *Foundations for A Practical Theology of Ministry* (Nashville: Abingdon Press, 1985) 90

45. Rebecca S. Chopp in "Educational Process, Feminist Practice" in *Christian Century*, February 1-8, 1995, 111-115

46. "Once to Every Man and Nation" in *Pilgrim Hymnal*. (New York: The Pilgrim Press, 1931, renewed 1986).

Bibliography

Altman, Nathaniel. *Sacred Trees*. San Francisco: Sierra Club Books, 1994.

Budge, E. A. Wallis. *Cleopatra's Needles and other Egyptian Obelisks*. London: Religious Tract Society, 1926.

Dibner, Bern. *Moving the Obelisks: A Chapter in Engineering History*. Cambridge: MIT Press, 1970.

Durant, Will. *Caesar and Christ*. New York: Simon and Schuster,1944.

Engelbach, Reginald. *The Problem of the Obelisks*. New York: George H. Doran, 1923.

Fasola, Umberto M. *Peter and Paul in Rome*. Rome: Vision, 1980.

Ferrari, Oreste. *Masterpieces of the Vatican*. London: Thames and Hudson, Ltd., 1971.

Habachi, Labib. *The Obelisks of Egypt: Skyscrapers of the Past*. Cairo: American University Press, 1984.

Hart, George. *Egyptian Myths*. London: British Museum Press, 1990.

Holmes, Urban Tigner. *Ministry and Imagination*. New York : Seabury Press, 1981.

Holmes, Urban Tigner. *Spirituality for Ministry*. New York: Harper & Row, 1982.

Humphrey, John H. *Roman Circuses: Arenas for Chariot Racing*. Berkeley: University of California Press, 1985.

Iversen, Erik. *Obelisks in Exile*. Copenhagen: Gad, 1968.

Parker, John Henry. *The Archaeology of Rome. Vol. IV. Obelisks*. Oxford: J. Park and Co., 1874.

Poling, James N. and Donald E. Miller. *Foundations for A Practical Theology of Ministry*. Nashville: Abingdon Press, 1985.

Roullet, Anne. *The Egyptian and Egyptianizing Monuments of Imperial Rome*. Leiden: E. J. Brill, 1972.

Scott, Jamie, ed. *Sacred Places and Profane Spaces: Essays in the Geographies of Judaism, Christianity, and Islam*. New York: Greenwood Press, 1991.

Swan, James A. *The Power of Place: Sacred Ground in Natural and Human Environments*. Bath, U.K.: Gateway Books, 1993.

Sypher, Wylie. *Four Stages of Renaissance Style*. Garden City: Doubleday and Co., 1956.

Tompkins, Peter. *The Magic of Obelisks*. New York: Harper and Row, 1981.

Vatsyayan, Kapila. *Concepts of Space Ancient and Modern*. New Delhi: Indira Gandhi National Centre for the Arts, 1991.

Walker, Barbara C. *The Woman's Encyclopedia of Myths and Secrets*. San Francisco: Harper and Row, 1983.

ABOUT THE AUTHOR

After his first experiences in Italy, Michael Bausch took more than 20 groups of travelers with him to enjoy the art, architecture, antiquities, and culture of that country. This led him into studies he would later share with others by teaching seminars, summer sessions, and university courses and preaching illustrated sermons.

He is the author of *Silver Screen, Sacred Story: Using Multimedia in Worship*; *Feeding Imaginations: Worship That Engages*; and *Saturday Morning and Other Stories*. He also co-edited *A Media Sourcebook* and *Everflowing Streams: Songs For Worship*.

About the Publisher

Image Source, which is owned and operated by Fred Noer, provides writing and editing services and black-and-white photographic images of landscapes. For more information, go to www.frednoer.com.

www.ingramcontent.com/pod-product-compliance
Lightning Source LLC
Chambersburg PA
CBHW072214170526
45158CB00002BA/598